CW01095836

THE D-DAY TRAINING
POCKET MANUAL 1944

Edited by Chris McNab

CASEMATE

Oxford & Philadelphia

Published in Great Britain and
the United States of America in 2019 by
CASEMATE PUBLISHERS
The Old Music Hall, 106–108 Cowley Road, Oxford OX4 1JE, UK
1950 Lawrence Road, Havertown, PA 19083, USA

Introduction and chapter introductory texts by Chris McNab
© Casemate Publishers 2019

Hardback Edition: ISBN 978-1-61200-733-5
Digital Edition: ISBN 978-1-61200-734-2

A CIP record for this book is available from the British Library

Printed in the Czech Republic by FINIDR, s.r.o.

The information and advice contained in the documents in this book is solely
for historical interest and does not constitute advice. The publisher accepts no
liability for the consequences of following any of the advice in this book.

For a complete list of Casemate titles, please contact:

CASEMATE PUBLISHERS (UK)
Telephone (01865) 241249
Fax (01865) 794449
Email: casemate-uk@casematepublishers.co.uk
www.casematepublishers.co.uk

CASEMATE PUBLISHERS (US)
Telephone (610) 853-9131
Fax (610) 853-9146
Email: casemate@casematepublishers.com
www.casematepublishers.com

CONTENTS

INTRODUCTION

Of all the great turning points in history, when the fates of millions of people and entire continents hung in the balance, the D-Day invasion of north-western Europe on 6 June 1944 must surely rank amongst the most significant. Had the Allies failed in successfully establishing the second front – a distinct possibility given the strength of the Axis forces they faced – then the liberation of Western Europe could have been almost indefinitely postponed, if not removed, as a strategic possibility.

Germany was certainly imperilled on other fronts, the most looming threat coming from a surging Red Army on the Eastern Front, its offensive momentum snowballing after the German catastrophes at Stalingrad in the winter of 1942–43 and at Kursk in July 1943. But if the Wehrmacht had quashed the Allied landings at Normandy, such a defeat would potentially have allowed the redeployment of major German forces from the West back out to the East and Italy, to hold back the tides there. Had this been the case, Hitler might not have achieved the vast Third Reich of which he dreamt, but there is the perfect possibility that he could have held onto large swathes of Western Europe already under occupation.

The actual planning for what would be called Operation *Overlord*, the invasion of north-west Europe (the actual D-Day landings were code-named Operation *Neptune*), began in sketchy outline back in January 1943. The Allied political leaders and Combined Chiefs of Staff at the strategic Casablanca conference made a theoretical commitment to opening a second front in 1944, reinforced practically by creating the position of Chief of Staff to the Supreme Allied Commander (COSSAC) and laying the political conditions for the French National Committee for Liberation.

Military planners now began vast feasibility and force studies, with a particular focus on the best location for the landings. This choice had a challenging set of criteria. First, the coastal geography had to allow the physical landing of tens of thousands of men, hundreds of vehicles, and acres of logistical supplies. Second, but related, was the requirement to secure a major port for offloading supplies in the appropriate volumes. (The 36 divisions that would eventually be deployed into France required the ingress of about 20,000 tons of supplies and equipment every single day to maintain the offensive momentum.) Similarly, the landing zone also needed a good road network in the immediate interior, to facilitate the push of logistics forward once the breakout began. Third, the landing beaches and the hinterland beyond had to be within the combat radius of Allied bombers, fighters and ground-attack aircraft flying from the southern UK, not just allowing for there-

and-back journeys but providing as much loiter time as possible. Finally, the landing areas naturally needed to be at weak points in the enemy defence, with the best opportunities for delaying the deployment of reserves to the beachheads.

The point of entry was eventually decided upon as the stretch of Normandy between Cherbourg to the west and Le Havre to the east, this location winning out over Brittany and the Cotentin peninsula (too vulnerable to being cut-off by German counter-attacks) and the Pas-de-Calais (closest to the UK, but most heavily defended). The outline plan was approved at the Quadrant conference in Quebec in August 1943, although by this time the sheer scale of the operation was becoming apparent, leading to a requested increase (approved in January 1944) of invasion divisions from five to eight, including three airborne divisions.

Full and detailed planning began in earnest in February 1944, with the formation of the Supreme Headquarters Allied Expeditionary Force (SHAEF), headed by US General Dwight D. Eisenhower. *Overlord* would be conducted by the 21st Army Group headed by British General Bernard Montgomery, its two major force components being the US First Army (Lieutenant General Omar Bradley) and the British Second Army (Lieutenant General Sir Miles Dempsey).

Given the high stakes of the D-Day landings, the preparations for this event were of dizzying magnitude and complexity. Some 3 million personnel of all services would be committed to the operation, including 1.2 million US servicemen transported across the Atlantic into the UK. During May 1944 alone, 1.9 million tons of invasion supplies were shipped in Britain. A total of 7,000 ships and landing craft were assembled, and in the first month of operations in Normandy more than 171,500 vehicles were transferred into the theatre, all of which had to be assembled, maintained and allocated to units in the run-up to the invasion.

What is truly extraordinary, given the vast scale of the build-up, was that its eventual destination was kept concealed from the Germans, and indeed from millions of Allied service personnel, until its revelation was necessary, often mere hours before debarkation. The deception operation, code-named Operation *Bodyguard*, could not disguise the fact that an invasion was coming, somewhere. The Germans, recognising this fact for some time, had not only erected the formidable coastal defences known as the Atlantic Wall – although these were far from completion by June 1944 – but they also had considerable numbers of divisions in western France. The *Oberbefehlshaber West* (OB West; Commander-in-Chief West), Generalfeldmarschall Gerd von Rundstedt, had at his disposal the forces of Army Group B (Generalfeldmarschall Erwin Rommel) between Saint Nazaire and the Belgian coast. The intended landing beaches in Normandy fell on the army boundary between the Seventh Army to the south and the Fifteenth Army to the north, the latter being numerically stronger, with more divisions, and qualitatively stronger, in terms of combat-experienced formations. Yet the vast majority of the Fifteenth Army was north of the River Seine, its troops expecting to repel an Allied invasion in the Pas-de-Calais. In total these two armies presented 25 coastal divisions, 16 infantry and airborne divisions, 10 armoured and mechanized divisions and 7 reserve divisions, an enormous on-paper strength that would dwarf whatever the Allies could land by ship. Famously, a dispute arose between Hitler and Rommel on one side and Rundstedt and General Leo Geyr von Schweppenburg (commander of Panzer Group West) on the other. The former pair advocated that armour formations be moved up to the beachheads, to repel enemy forces immediately as they landed, while the latter argued that the reserve should be held back and used to form the counter-attack once it became clear where the Allied forces had landed. In the end, the decision was fudged and the German armoured forces were distributed poorly to respond to what was to come.

Given the disposition of German forces, it was imperative that the Allies, through a combination of deception and force, keep the troops of the Fifteenth Army in the north, away from the Normandy beaches. Operation *Bodyguard* accomplished this masterfully, essentially convincing the German high command that any attack in Normandy would be a ruse, deflecting from the real onslaught against the Pas-de-Calais. The Allies created the appearance of two entirely notional invasion forces, the First US Army Group (FUSAG) under General George S. Patton Jr. in the south-east of England and the Fourth Army in Scotland under Lieutenant General Sir A. F. A. N. Thorne. Both were shell forces; instead of containing thousands of troops and armoured vehicles their presence was recreated by small units, creative signals broadcasts, fake supply dumps and fabric and wood dummy vehicles, for the benefit of German aerial reconnaissance. The deception, combined with dozens of other activities, compelled the Germans to keep major units in both the Pas-de-Calais and Norway. As an indicator of the persuasion achieved, the German Fifteenth Army basically wasted seven weeks in their positions north of the Seine even after the Allied landings.

As well as effective deception, the other factor very much in the Allies' favour was its undoubted superiority in air power. The air assets available were contained mainly in the Allied Expeditionary Air Force (AEAF) under the command of Sir Trafford Leigh-Mallory. The AEAF contained two major tactical air formations, the RAF Second Tactical Air Force and the USAF Ninth Air Force. In the immediate weeks before D-Day, however, the combined muscle of RAF Bomber Command and the US Eighth Air Force were brought under SHAEF command at Eisenhower's personal request. Between 1 April and 5 June 1944, these and other aircraft delivered some 195,00 tons of bombs on priority logistical targets around France, such as railroad marshalling yards, bridges, industrial units and radar positions. This effort was part of the 'Transportation Plan', designed in large part by Professor Solly Zuckerman, an advisor to the Air Ministry, and intended to isolate the D-Day battlefield from German resupply and reinforcements. In this it was highly successful, fending off criticism from some quarters that the RAF and USAAF bomber fleets had been unnecessarily diverted away from their important strategic bombing roles. On D-Day itself, the air operations around and beyond the beachheads were supported by some 9,500 Allied aircraft, an aerial armada that the meagre German forces in the region were utterly unable to resist.

The efforts to assemble the invasion land army and air force were more than matched, even surpassed, by the Herculean achievements of the naval forces. The Allied naval forces committed to D-Day totalled some 7,000 ships and 195,000 personnel. The role of the naval units was not only to transport the invasion troops, and land them on the beaches via various specialist landing craft, but also to provide an immense preparatory bombardment of the enemy shoreline and to ensure that logistics were pumped into the beachhead and inland advance at a rate as fast as demand.

After a period of delays owing to adverse weather conditions, the D-Day operation was finally launched on 6 June 1944. The initial fleet of 4,000 transport ships, escorted by 600 warships, crossed the Channel in the hours of morning darkness, carrying 176,000 men. Five beaches had been assigned for the invaders, code-named from west to east: 'Utah' and 'Omaha' designated for the US First Army, and 'Gold', 'Juno' and 'Sword' for the British Second Army. Overhead flew a vast armada of transport aircraft and gliders, carrying the airborne soldiers of the US 82nd and 101st Airborne Divisions and the British 6th Airborne Division. From 0200 hrs, the American troops were dropped/landed inland around positions west of Utah Beach, while at the same time the British paratroopers went in north-east of Caen. Both airborne strikes had roughly the same purpose – to secure the flanks of the invasion and to seize key objectives that the Germans might use for their counter-attacks, such as bridges and gun batteries. Although the confusion of the night-time drop, plus heavy German anti-aircraft fire, resulted in many of the paratroopers being scattered well away from their intended locations, they still managed to cause great disruption in the German rear, confusing the Germans initially as to the nature and direction of the threat and attacking targets of opportunity.

The German defenders were in little doubt as to what was heading their way when, at 0315 hrs, hundreds of Allied aircraft began softening up the landing areas with thousands of tons of bombs. The US and British tactical air forces roamed far and wide over the battlefield and beyond throughout the day, making every German attempt to move up reinforcements a tortuous and casualty-heavy experience, particularly for armoured and mechanized troops. Then, at 0550 hrs, the warships of the invasion fleet were close enough to deliver an awesome and terrifying preparatory bombardment, the guns of 600 escort vessels letting fly with everything from rocket batteries to battleship main guns.

At 0630 hrs, the first infantry landings went ashore on the beaches. Each beach would have its own unique story, its own tragedies (see Chapter 4 for more details of the specific beach landings). There was resistance at each landing, but to varying degrees. Thus, for example, at Gold Beach the British managed to establish themselves fairly quickly and pushed out beyond, while at the American Omaha Beach hundreds of assault troops were massacred on the shoreline, and for a time it appeared that here the landing might fail. Yet ultimately every landing zone was seized by the end of the day. In fact, D-Day was an arduous but crowning success. Total casualties, dead and wounded, were just over 10,000 men, but this was actually far lower than had been predicted. Balanced against the casualties was the fact that 75,000 British and Canadian troops and 57,500 US troops had been landed, secured the beachheads, and had begin pushing out into occupied France. The Germans had been unable to prevent the Allies establishing the second front, a failure that secured the fate of the Third Reich.

This book brings together a fascinating collection of documents that would feed into the planning and thinking about D-Day. Because of the secrecy surrounding the operation, there are no specific 'D-Day manuals' as such. Yet the key themes of D-Day – naval gunfire support, airborne deployments, amphibious landings, close-air support, engineer operations – had been studied and refined in depth prior to June 1944. These manuals drew on a wide range of theoretical understanding and practical experience. By presenting them here, we gain a better sense of what it took to plan and execute D-Day, both from the higher levels of operational thinking down to the combat actions of the individual soldier.

CHAPTER I

INTELLIGENCE, PLANNING AND PREPARATION

Most of the planning and preparation for the D-Day invasion was done in the six months between January and June 1944. In this intensive period, the Allied forces not only had to define and collect forces sufficient to accomplish the task in hand, but they also had to gather all available intelligence about the defences that they would face on the Normandy coastline. By spring 1944 the Allies had already made major and successful amphibious landings, especially in the Pacific theatre but also in North Africa (Operation *Torch*, 8 November 1942), Sicily (Operation *Husky*, 9 July 1943) and Italy (four separate landings between September 1943 and January 1944). These experiences provided many lessons learned, and their ultimate success was encouraging, but there were plenty of reasons to be cautious. The landings at Anzio on 22 January 1944, for example, were initially successful, but command decisions led to the Allied forces becoming essentially trapped around the beachhead for weeks, under German counter-attacks and taking heavy casualties. There was also the sobering lesson of the Dieppe Raid (Operation *Jubilee*) in August 1942, launched primarily by Canadian forces with the express purpose of testing out German coastal defences. Within just 10 hours, 60 per cent of the raiding force were casualties in a disastrous action.

A priority for the Allied intelligence services was, therefore, to assess properly the level of threat posed by the units and defences along the Normandy coastline. Some of the information gathered is shown in our first source, *German Coastal Defenses*, publishing by the US military intelligence service in June 1943. Here the analysts present insight into the specific types of obstacles and threats on German beaches and the surrounding areas. Construction of Hitler's 'Atlantic Wall' – a chain of coastal fortifications and defences stretching sporadically from the Netherlands to Spain – began in the summer of 1942. Although it led to some formidable stretches of defences, investment ran behind need for much of 1942 and 1943. In the autumn of 1943, however, the great German Field Marshal Erwin Rommel was given responsibility for accelerating the building process and strengthening the defences, which he did with gusto. By the time that the Allies landed on 6 June 1944, Omaha beach alone had 3,700 beach obstacles.

German Coastal Defenses (1943)

Section III: BEACH OBSTACLES

8. GENERAL

The critical points of Europe's Atlantic coast are, of course, those beaches which are suitable for major landing operations. Germany's maximum effort in men, materials, and weapons on her Western Front has been directed toward the fortification of these potential gateways to the interior.

Forbidden zones have been defined by the Germans, and their inhabitants have been evacuated therefrom, not only to facilitate the organization and construction of defenses but also to prevent the native population from joining or assisting any landing forces. Seaside homes and other buildings along the coast have been razed to provide fields of fire, or space for the construction of reinforced concrete forts, ammunition dumps, and gun emplacements.

Those buildings that have been allowed to stand near the beaches have been incorporated in the defenses. Many attractive villas are still deceptively innocent and peaceful in appearance, but only the exteriors remain the same. The interiors of some have been converted into steel-and-concrete emplacements, and they have been armed with guns of varying sizes. Many of the houses have not been fortified so elaborately, but have been turned into effective positions for smaller guns and machine guns by the filling-in of doors and windows with brick or concrete. Passages have been cut through continuous rows of fortified houses so that the occupying troops may pass from one to another without being exposed to observation and fire from the beach. Corner houses which command stretches of roads and intersections have likewise been converted into emplacements for weapons.

The sea walls and the promenades or boardwalks along the beach fronts have also been fortified by the installation of emplacements from which guns could be brought to bear on the beach and the water beyond. In some places the dunes are no longer mere heaps of sand dotted with bunch grass. They have been hollowed out, and reinforced concrete shelters and emplacements have been built within them. Such concrete works are occupied by antiaircraft and heavy gun crews, and by infantry units that would come out to engage landing forces.

As for the beach proper, the Germans have devised a variety of obstacles of more or less conventional type. These will be discussed in detail in this section.

[. . .]

9. UNDERWATER OBSTACLES

a. Stakes

In the shallow water off beaches with gentle slopes, the Germans have embedded rows of steel stakes and wooden logs. They are set at an angle, their upper ends pointing outward from the beach. Submerged barbed wire and mines may be used in conjunction with these obstacles, which are intended to trap landing boats, or personnel who may be compelled to leave their boats to wade ashore.

b. Booms

As obstacles against landing craft, light booms of simple construction are placed by the Germans in front of good landing beaches. They consist, usually, of conical buoys, linked by wire rope that runs through the tops and bases of the buoys. Rafts are similarly employed. Explosives and warning devices may be affixed to these booms.

10. BARBED WIRE

a. General

This part of the discussion deals with German wire technique, as observed in The Netherlands, Belgium, and France. On the beaches, barbed wire is usually erected in straight lines, parallel to the shore and in front of fortified areas. In the spaces between fortified areas the lines of wire jut out at right angles toward the sea.

The depth of wire obstacles around emplacements and fortified areas varies with the topography and importance of the site. In some places it may be 30 to 60 yards; in other positions the depth may range from 70 to 130 yards, or may go up to 200 yards. Generally, the distance from the outside edge of wire to the nearest pillbox or other firing position is not less than 30 yards.

Dense entanglements are installed in gullies and in the crevices of cliffs, whence the wire may continue as single fences along the top margin of the cliffs. The entanglements usually begin to thin out half-way up the side of gullies. In front of these obstacles the Germans sometimes erect small-mesh wire, apparently to slow up the employment of bangalore torpedoes.

The Germans often use wire to fence off all sides of a minefield. These fences consist of a single row of pickets with five or six strands of wire. In conjunction with road blocks, a wire entanglement or fence is employed on each side of the road, and the gap between is closed by movable gates of various types. Concrete walls and other more substantial types of barriers are now replacing wire entanglements as road blocks in many places. A thin belt of wire is usually erected outside of antitank ditches. Wire is employed on practically all wall barriers and concrete emplacements, which often have iron staples in them for the stringing of apron and other types of entanglements.

A new type of German barbed wire now in use is thicker than ordinary wire, is made of a noncorrosive metal, and is rectangular in section. It has three-quarter-inch barbs at intervals of 4 inches.

b. Specific Types

Some details of specific types of wire obstacles in The Netherlands, Belgium, and France are listed below. The dimensions are approximate.

(1) *Knife rests.*—Knife rests, or cheval-de-frise obstacles, strung with wire, have been observed on beaches above high-water mark. Some examples consist of four trestles connected by a cross bar. The dimensions are as follows:

Height _ _ _ _ _ _ _ 4 feet

Span of trestle legs _ _ _ _ _ _ _ 4 feet

Distance between trestles _ _ _ _ _ _ _ 4 to 5 feet

Length of four-trestle unit _ _ _ _ _ _ _ 16 to 20 feet

(2) *Apron fences.*—These may be single or double aprons. Screw pickets or angle-irons embedded in concrete to a depth of about 18 inches are used to hold them. Sometimes a coil of concertina may be placed under double-apron fences. Another variation is to place a coil of concertina on the tops of such fences. The dimensions are as follows:

Height _ _ _ _ _ _ _ 4 to 5 feet

Height (with coil on top) _ _ _ _ _ _ _ 7 to 8 feet

Width _ _ _ _ _ _ _ Up to 30 feet

(3) *Vertical fences.*—Vertical fences are invariably installed in two or three lines, 4 to 8 feet apart. Each fence has five or six strands of wire, and is 4 to 6 feet high. Wooden posts, angle-irons, and screw pickets are used as supports. Various types of entanglements and mines are often used in the spaces between fences.

(4) *Concertina fences.*—Single, double, or triple coils of concertina are used with angle-irons or screw pickets. Triple coils are often affixed to the rails of the promenades that are so common along the beaches of western Europe.

(5) *Trip fences.*—Trip wires in diagonal or diamond-shaped trace are frequently found in front of major obstacles, usually between the high-water mark and the first barbed-wire entanglement, or they are erected in fields before main defensive positions or obstacles. Their dimensions are as follows:

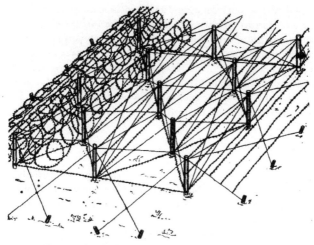

Figure 7. Standard German barbed-wire obstacle in depth.

Height _ _ _ _ _ _ _ 4 to 6 inches

Length of each diagonal or diamond-shaped trace _ _ _ _ _ _ _ 4 to 6 feet

Width of whole obstacle _ _ _ _ _ _ _ 12 to 20 feet

(6) *Alarm wires.*—There is evidence that many wires have some form of alarm device connected to them, such as grenades, small explosive charges, and insulated live wire, which would ring a bell if cut.

(7) *Electrified wire.*—Electrified barbed wire, held by insulators to pickets, has been reported, but it is not likely to be encountered on a large scale.

(8) *Combined fences.*—A typical combined fence may consist of the following units in the order given: a trip wire, a trestle fence or knife rest, and (10 to 20 yards farther back) an apron fence. The total depth of such a combination may be 30 to 60 yards. On the sea fronts of towns, the usual practice is to have an apron or knife-rest fence on the beach, and a concertina or apron fence on the top of the sea wall and promenade.

[. . .]

11. MINEFIELDS

a. General

During the North African campaign the Germans made great use of minefields and developed minefield technique to a high degree of effectiveness. They have applied this experience widely in western Europe, where they have had plenty of time to lay out fields behind important beaches and in their rearward defenses. The German Army teaches that mines are a very powerful defensive weapon, and that their skilled employment in combination with other weapons strengthens defense, especially when the defender is considerably inferior in numbers. The Germans also teach that the employment of mines must be under strict control and in the hands of well-trained, courageous troops. Their basic doctrine prescribes the use of minefields in advanced positions, in the vicinity of the main line of resistance, and in the depth of the position.

[. . .]

The principles which guide the Germans in selecting a minefield location are essentially the same as U.S. principles. Maximum use is made of natural and artificial barriers to compel vehicles to cross the minefield. Roadways are usually mined at points where vehicles cannot detour, the aim being to cause the cratering of the road and damage to vehicles. Mines are also used wherever it is desired to augment the difficulties of passing natural or artificial obstacles.

Extensive use is made of mines in preparing a hasty defense against counterattack. Under such conditions, because of lack of time for proper burial and concealment, the mines are generally not concealed, but are laid on the ground surface until there is an opportunity to bury them. When the ground is covered with snow, land mines may not be buried until the melting of the snow makes concealment necessary.

Although standard patterns may be prescribed in training pamphlets, there is considerable variation in the actual layout of German minefields. The Germans leave gaps in minefields for their own use, but normally they will place a small field about 50 paces behind the gap to act as a stopper. By the use of dummy mines, the Germans leave paths for the passage of their own vehicles. Tellermines are normally used to form antitank minefields, whereas heavy antitank mines are used for road blocks.

b. Minefield Layouts

    (1) *Tellermine minefield patterns.*—

        (a) *Method of spacing.*—The measurements which establish the location of individual mines in a field are ordinarily made by pacing. Consequently, considerable variation from the intended pattern may be encountered. For "close spacing," the interval varies from 3 to 5 yards; none is less than 2 yards. If spaced at 3-yard centers, the detonation of one mine will invariably detonate the one next to it. In "open spacing," Tellermines are laid 10 yards apart.

According to a German document, the distance between Tellermines, center to center, should be 5 paces (13 feet) when laid in the ground, or 10 paces (26 feet) when laid on the surface.

In North Africa, minefields of 6 rows have been found in which German Tellermines and Italian B-2 mines have been laid in alternate rows; individual mines were laid from 5 to 8 yards apart. These mines also have been found installed together in a haphazard manner throughout an entire minefield. In some minefields in Cyrenaica, Tellermines were laid on 9-foot centers. In one instance, the firing of 1 mine set off a field of 980 mines, set 9 feet apart, by sympathetic detonation.

(b) *Hasty minefield.*—A layout for a hasty minefield is shown in figure 8. It has panels 30 paces across the front by 30 paces in depth, or approximately 80 by 80 feet. Each panel contains 12 mines. The resulting density is 1 mine for each 6½ feet of front, and thus would be classified as open-spaced. The panels are repeated side by side to cover the desired length of front.

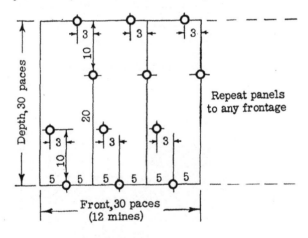

NOTE: All dimensions in paces

Figure 8. Hasty minefield pattern (open spacing).

(c) *Deliberate minefield.*—The layout for a somewhat more deliberate type of minefield is shown in figure 9. This is also open-spaced. The panel is 30 paces across the front by 40 paces in depth, or approximately 80 feet by 105 feet. It contains 24 mines, giving a density of 1 mine per meter (3¼ feet of front). These panels are combined to form staggered patterns of 3 panels each. Each panel

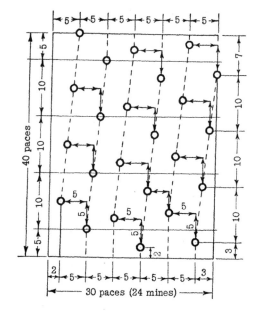

NOTE: All dimensions in paces

Figure 9. Deliberate minefield pattern (open spacing).

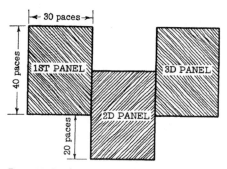

Figure 10. Panel arrangement of deliberate minefield.

is offset 20 paces (52½ feet) from the adjacent panels, as shown in figure 10. These patterns of 3 panels each may be further combined to form a more extensive minefield layout.

(d) *Variation of deliberate minefield.*—In a report dated September 1942, from North Africa, it is stated that a variation in the pacing of

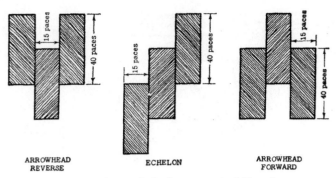

ARROWHEAD
REVERSE

ECHELON

ARROWHEAD
FORWARD

Figure 11. Three methods of arranging minefield panels.

the deliberate minefield shown in figure 9 was found. The variation consisted of the horizontal and vertical coordinates being 6 paces and the minimum spacing between mines being 7 paces. When open spacing was employed, the above dimensions were doubled.

Another variation of this more deliberate minefield is a panel having close spacing and measuring 15 paces across the front by 40 paces in depth, or approximately 40 feet by 105 feet. It contains 24 mines, giving a density of 2 mines per meter (3¼ feet) of front. These panels are normally combined in groups of 3 in arrowhead reverse, in echelon, or in arrowhead forward formation, as shown in figure 11. These groups of 3 panels each are further combined to form large minefields or a part of an extensive layout, as shown in figure 12 (1).

(e) *Extensive minefield.*—An extensive minefield layout may combine groups of open-spaced and close-spaced panels (see fig. 12 (1)). A minimum distance of 50 paces (131 feet) between fields is maintained.

Figure 12 (2) shows a German-Italian plan of an extensive minefield in which the deliberate minefield pattern was used. The main minefield area (1) with mine zones (2) laid in patterns is bordered in the front and rear with barbed wire (3) and with other barbed wire (4) running irregularly through the minefield for the purpose of deception. In front of the main minefield (1) is a minefield (5) of scattered mines marked in front with a broken line of barbed wire (6). The gaps (7) are intended for deception. A strongpoint (8) is located to the rear of the main minefield.

(f) *Road blocks.*—Tellermines may be used in road blocks, alone or in conjunction with artificial barriers. The interval between mines is about 1 pace (2½ feet), and slightly less than this between rows. Thus four rows, as shown in figure 13, give a density of one mine to each 7½ inches of width in the roadway. When the Germans

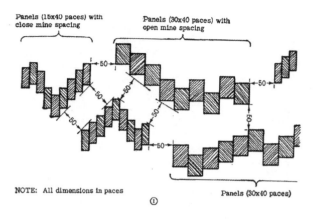

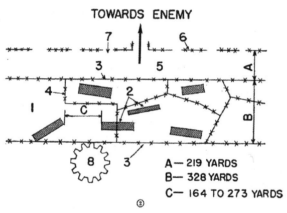

Figure 12. Extensive layout of minefields.

mine a road, yet continue to use it for their own needs, one-half of the road is left unmined. Detours which the Germans have used to bypass their own road blocks may be heavily mined when the area is given up to the advance of opposing forces. If the nature of the road surface permits, mines are buried. Mines are sometimes laid indiscriminately on the shoulders of the roads. In North Africa, railroad tracks leading out of towns have been mined as in figure 14. Other road blocks have been found where mines were laid in a few "chuck" holes in the roads, while other holes were left empty. Of course, all holes had to be carefully examined. For 10 kilometers (about 6¼ miles) south of Agedabia, road blocks were laid at all kilometer stones, which were used as markers.

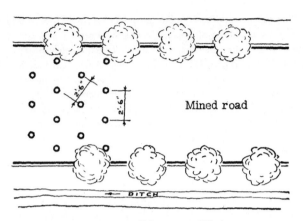

Figure 13. Tellermine road block.

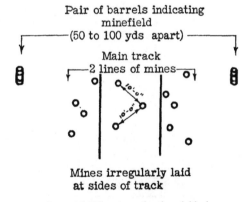

Figure 14. Tellermine railroad-track block.

(2) *Heavy antitank mine fields.*—The German heavy antitank mine is normally used to form antitank road blocks on main lines of communication. The road blocks formed by these mines usually contain between 15 and 20 mines laid in 1 of 2 patterns, as follows:

    (a) In a line diagonally across the road, 20 mines occupying about 100 yards of road.

    (b) In a checkerboard pattern, with the mines placed 6½ to 8 feet apart arid each row of mines covering the gaps of the preceding row. The depth of the minefield may be 15 to 20 yards or more. In some cases Tellermines have been found mixed with heavy mines.

(3) *Antipersonnel minefields.*—The antipersonnel mines are placed in fields and are on occasion very precisely located by means of standard layout equipment. This equipment consists of an equilateral triangle made up of 10 rings, each 40 centimeters (15¾ inches) in internal diameter, and 18 cords, each 4.4 meters (14.43 feet) long. (See fig. 15.) Each side of this triangle, formed by the joining of the cords and rings, is, therefore, 43.3 feet long and is made up of 3 cord lengths and 4 rings. The triangle is laid out on the ground with 1 edge along a base line, and an antipersonnel mine is planted in each ring. The triangle is then turned through 60 degrees on the corner of the triangle farthest from the base line, and more mines are laid at each ring. (See fig. 16.) This procedure is repeated to form some such continuous field as shown in figure 17.

The field as shown is registered for map-record purposes by extending the base line 100 meters (328 feet) rearward and marking it with pickets at 20-meter (65.6-foot) intervals (Points P1, P2, P3, P4, P5, and P6), except that for safety the point P6 is set back 2 meters (6.6 feet) from the corner mine, making the interval from PS to P6 only 18 meters (59 feet). The Point P1 is registered on two reference points HP1 and HP2, and the azimuth of the extended base line P1 to P6 is recorded.

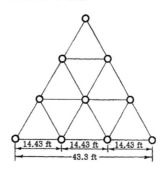

Figure 15. Equilateral triangle layout for antipersonnel minefields.

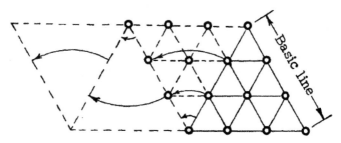

Figure 16. Method of rotating equilateral triangle layout for antipersonnel minefields.

(4) *Minefields in a defile.*—The mines are laid out in regular rows from a line based on outstanding existing features which lie on the forward edge of the proposed minefield. The interval between rows varies between 2 feet 4 inches and 5 feet. The number of rows is not fixed, but the minefield is designed to give a density of at least one mine to 1 foot 2 inches of front. The mines are carefully concealed. Au accurate record is kept of the extent of the minefield and of any gaps which may have been left for the Germans' own use.

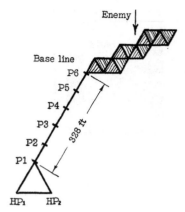

Figure 17. Continuous antipersonnel minefield.

c. Minefield Records

Minefields are mapped on a scale of 1:2,500, and the complete scheme is transferred to a 1:10,000 map.

d. Marking

Minefields laid in advance of an enemy approach are marked by holes, sticks, branches, or wires as warning to German troops. A report of a minefield at Ben Temrad states that mines were laid at very irregular spacing, but always in or near a vehicular track. The mines laid across the vehicular tracks were generally marked with small stone cairns at the corners of the fields. Mines were also laid along tracks, and these seemed to be marked by cairns at either end of the mined sections.

In May 1942, an order issued by the German 90th Light Division stated that the existing methods of marking minefields were inadequate. Minefields were to be marked either by a strong wire fence 1 meter (39 inches) high or stone walls 40 cm (16 inches) high. However, substitute materials such as barrels, concertina wire, tin cans, derelict vehicles, etc., might be used. In a report from Agedabia, a perimeter minefield, without markings, was located 20 yards behind the perimeter wire. Mines laid on roads or railroad tracks in North Africa were usually found installed close to some easily identifiable landmark, such as a kilometer stone, track junction, or a small stone cairn. Minefields and road blocks were also found marked by a 40-gallon oil drum, usually with a patch of red paint and holes in the top which marked routes past the minefields.

In May 1942, an order issued by the German 15th Armored Division described minefield-gap identifying signboards (see fig. 18) in red and white which were to be mounted on posts 3 feet 6 inches to 5 feet high. In the

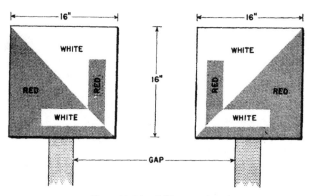

Figure 18. Minefield gap signboards.

northern sector of the El Alamein line, minefield gaps were found which were marked by luminous tubes 1 inch long placed on top of the mines. They marked a route for patrols and were visible 3 yards away. Gaps have been reported to be 7 to 10 yards wide. Often the front edge of minefields is not marked, but the rear edge is usually marked by some form of fence, such as a trip wire on short pickets. Occasionally the rear edge of a minefield has been found unmarked. A common marking for minefields is a single row of concertina wire along the center of the minefield and parallel to the rows of mines. In a large minefield there may be several unmarked rows of mines along the front, a row of concertina wire, more rows of mines, then another row of concertina wire, and so on, with a row of concertina wire marking the rear edge of the minefield. Only one case has been reported of continuous wire running irregularly within a minefield.

e. German Conclusions on Minefield Practice

The Germans have drawn the following conclusions from their experiences with minefields:

(1) *Minefield layout plans.*—Accurate minefield plans are extremely important, since the unit employed in laying the land mines may not be the one to take them up.

(2) *Minefield reports.*—Prompt reports, accompanied by layout plans of all minefields, should be submitted to designated higher authority. If this is done, the publication of adequate warning will prevent losses of men and vehicles in their own minefields.

(3) *Temporary nature of minefields.*—Minefields should always be viewed as temporary, to be taken up again as our own troops advance. For this reason it is desirable to keep the troops engaged in land-mining in the section where

they have laid fields, so that they may remove the mines, if necessary, which they themselves set out.

(4) *Minefields behind water obstacles.*—In planting a minefield behind a water obstacle, the mines should be laid close to the water's edge. If mines are located several yards back, it is possible for the enemy to land personnel skilled in neutralizing them.

12. ANTITANK OBSTACLES AND ROAD BLOCKS

a. Dragon's Teeth and Ditches

One of the common forms of tank obstacles employed by the Germans is the "Dragon's Teeth," which consists of rows of reinforced, tapered concrete pedestals, cast monolithically on a common base. The concrete blocks vary in height up to 6 feet, and they are designed to immobilize a tank by bellying it. Fields of these blocks, used on a vast scale in the German West Wall and now installed also on the European coast, usually consist of four to eight rows in front of prepared positions. They are usually laid in straight lines to simplify artillery registration on them. In front of each of these fields the Germans normally dig an antitank ditch, at least 10 feet wide and, in exceptional cases, up to 60 feet wide.

Antitank ditches have also been dug at the approaches to coastal roads and key positions, and it is not unusual to find two ditches spaced only a few feet apart. Normally, these ditches have passages to permit the flow of single-line traffic. The rear walls of these ditches are usually revetted with concrete, earth, or brick, and some of them have steel rails projecting from the top.

Around strongly defended ports will be found antitank ditches 20 to 40 feet wide and up to 3 miles in length. They are usually laid in a zigzag course. Ditches of this length are most common in The Netherlands, but they are also found to a lesser extent in Belgium and France. In the construction of such a ditch in The Hague, the Germans demolished a row of three-story houses, more than a mile long.

These ditches are usually protected by a thin belt of wire, and by gun emplacements and pillboxes sited to enfilade the zigzag course of the ditch. Where streams or other water sources are available, the ditches have a sluice arrangement to keep them partially filled with water, or to flood them in the face of an attack.

Antitank ditches installed in front of defensive positions are usually 9 to 12 feet wide and up to 8 feet deep.

When employed thus, they are sited as follows:

(1) The ditches completely surround fortified positions, and radio-direction and other radio installations. Usually there is a thin belt of barbed

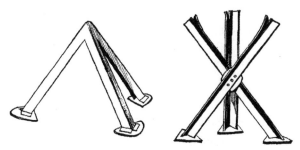

Figure 19. Types of steel cheval-de-frise trestles.

wire 10 to 20 yards in front of the ditch and a thicker belt about 50 yards to the rear of the ditch.

(2) The ditches are dug in front of fortified areas on beaches, behind beach wire, and at the foot of sand dunes.

(3) The ditches are dug in front of antitank walls and sea walls in coastal towns. They are usually without revetment, and may be dug 10 to 20 yards in front of the wall, or immediately in front of the wall.

b. Miscellaneous Obstacles

(1) *Chevaux-de-frise.*—Portable barriers of the cheval-de-frise type are commonly used by the Germans to block streets and important highway intersections. In some coastal places these obstacles are moved into position every night, evidently as a safeguard against commando raids. In other spots they are merely kept ready for placing during alerts. Two types of trestles for chevaux-de-frise are illustrated in figure 19.

(2) *Logs and rails.*—Logs and steel rails of varying heights are employed for making fixed and movable obstacles. Usually they are laid in "asparagus beds," the individual rails being spaced about 4 feet apart. Angle-iron frames with upright steel rails, set in pairs on a common base, are also laid in rows to form barriers. The example shown in figure 20 is more than 6 feet high. Various kinds of "swinging gate" obstacles are used in large numbers to block streets.

(3) *Wire obstacles.*—The Germans sometimes use concertina wire, disposed in depth, as a road block. They are also apt to conceal antitank and antipersonnel mines in these obstacles.

c. Walls and Promenades

(1) *Walls.*—At many points along the western European coast the Germans have built concrete walls to serve as antitank and antipersonnel obstacles. Such walls usually are placed to obstruct the ends of thoroughfares and other easy exits from beaches and harbors, and to block the approaches

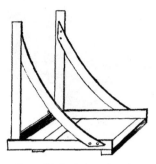

Figure 20. Angle-iron obstacle.

to key positions back of the beaches. Their dimensions are from 6 to 8 feet in thickness, and up to 20 feet in height. In various places in Belgium the Germans have installed behind these walls several types of antitank barriers which were removed from the Belgian defense lines of 1940. Both stationary and portable flame-throwers may also be encountered at these barriers.

Walls installed across the full width of a street are 6 to 8 feet high and may be from 8 to 11 feet thick. They are reinforced with concrete bars, the ends of which protrude from the tops of the walls to serve as pickets for barbed wire. The backs of these walls are generally sloped and may have fire steps from which to operate antitank guns. Walls of these same dimensions are sometimes constructed in V shapes at beach exits, especially on open beaches outside town limits. The point of the V is toward the sea. Some wall obstacles blocking the ends of thoroughfares opening on beaches have gaps in them to permit the passage of a single vehicle at one time. These obstacles are of two types. In the first, a section of wall is built at each side of the road, and the gap between them is closed, when necessary, by steel rails, girders, or gates that fit into sockets of the walls. The other type also has two sections of wall, but these are not directly opposite each other. They are "en chicane," or staggered, one section being as much as 16 feet behind the other, on the opposite side of the road. This arrangement compels a vehicle to slow down and zigzag to pass through.

Long stretches of concrete antitank walls are built along the rear edges of beaches and across the estuaries of streams, with gaps to permit the flow of water. Where the regular sea walls are not very high above the level of the sand, they are sometimes adapted as antitank barriers by excavating accumulated sand drifts and gravel from their seaward bases, or by heightening them with concrete. In some cases there is an outward bulge below the top front edge of these walls to make them more difficult to negotiate.

(2) *Promenades.*—The promenades or boardwalks so common along the beaches of The Netherlands, Belgium, and France must also be considered as

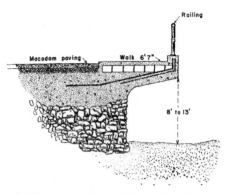

Figure 21. Cross section of typical European beach promenade.

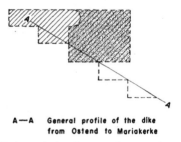

A—A General profile of the dike
from Ostend to Mariakerke

Figure 22. Antitank obstacle at top of promenade steps.

formidable obstacles, for infantry as well as for motor and armored vehicles. In many places they have been strengthened with reinforced concrete, and emplacements have been built into them. A typical example of such a promenade is shown in cross section in figure 21. Figure 22 shows how concrete blocks are used to discourage tanks from negotiating the stairway leading from a beach to the walk of a promenade.

d. Concealment and Deception

(1) *Camouflage and concealment.*—The Germans consider camouflage, concealment, and deception as very important and effective means of defense and have used these factors extensively in protecting coastal installations from ground as well as aerial observation. Troop shelters, pillboxes, hangars, dumps, and submarine and speedboat shelters have been constructed underground at all strategic points of the European coast. All open emplacements and the entrances of surface and underground installations have been skillfully disguised to add the protection of near-invisibility to the strength of reinforced

concrete. The camouflage varies to blend with the different types of terrain in German-occupied countries.

Forms of camouflage and concealment that have been noted are as follows:

(a) Garnished nets, turf, and seaweed are used to conceal concrete bunkers in northwest France.

(b) Tanks, probably worn out or obsolete, have been buried in the sands of the coastal regions of France and Belgium, the gun turrets painted to blend with the sand. Private houses in the same area have been converted into gun emplacements without altering their external appearances.

(c) Some underground machine-gun nests are concealed by a natural earth covering about 3 feet thick.

(d) Certain large shelters capable of accommodating approximately 500 men each are camouflaged green, gray, and black. (This is a fairly common German camouflage combination.)

(e) Extensive use has been made of nets to camouflage harbor installations.

(f) In northern France props have been used to conceal surface hangars and airfields in order to make them look like a village from the air. On one airfield was installed a light wood framework, painted to look like the side of a farm house. A false top was painted to represent tiles. A number of other false buildings, including a replica of a church, were also installed in the same place.

(g) Numerous camouflaged shelters for individual planes are also reported. In one place they were built among trees at the edge of a wood. The shelters were of wood, with gabled roofs, were covered with netting, and had trees painted on the doors. In other places individual hangars take the form of farm buildings and hollow haystacks. Many shelters have been camouflaged to look like sand dunes or have been buried in dunes in areas with long, sandy stretches.

(h) In rocky country, the combination of camouflage around concrete forts is likely to consist of rocks and nets. In one region where the sand has a yellowish tinge, the Germans have camouflaged their installations with yellow patterns, broken by green stripes.

(i) Pillboxes and light-gun emplacements are concealed with heaps of the rubble caused by Allied bombings.

(2) *Dummy installations.*—The use of dummy works and weapons is extensive and serves the double purpose of distracting aerial observation from actual defenses and of inducing the enemy to make wasteful attacks on barren

areas while the real defenses remain in operation. A common practice is to install dummy antiaircraft-gun positions and dummy guns, and even to simulate gun flashes in such positions, usually along lines of probable air approach. Sometimes real, mobile guns fire from the dummy positions in an effort to confound aerial reconnaissance. The practice is also extended to other types of artillery. Railway-gun turntables suspected of being faked have been noted in aerial reconnaissance. Dummy observation posts have also been reported. In some places that are heavily mined and wired but do not have a great many weapons, sham turrets and wooden guns are planted in barbed-wire lines.

Many dummy airfields exist along the coast of western Europe. Mock or disused planes and dummy buildings are installed on these fields, and at night they are likely to flash landing lights. From time to time the dummy aircraft are moved around to help fill out the impression of a field in actual operation.

Dummy installations are likely to be deliberately ostentatious or poorly camouflaged, in order to draw fire and distract attention from real and cleverly concealed fortifications.

13. HYPOTHETICAL LAYOUT OF BEACH DEFENSES

In order to offer a sample pattern of what the beach defense zone of western Europe is like, a hypothetical map of German beach defenses has been included in this section. The hypothetical map (fig. 23) is composite in style and is based on a study of known positions. It is typical of the defenses of a strategic landing beach with gentle gradient, backed by sand dunes.

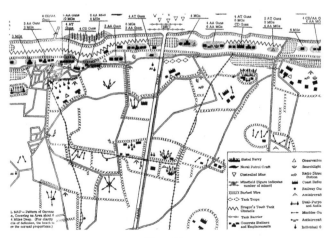

Figure 23.

The Manual of Combined Operations (1938) was compiled by the Training Division of the Naval Staff – and approved by the Admiralty, Army Council and Air Council – just before the onset of war in 1939, but its content is both prescient and relevant, and indeed the doctrine therein would have informed the planning for the D-Day operations. In essence the manual is a guidebook for the coordination of army, navy and air force assets in joint operations, principally the amphibious landing of forces on hostile shores. It covers the full range of operational considerations for such missions, including secrecy and deception, sea transport and landing craft, naval gunfire support, assaulting contested shores (by day and by night), beach organization and medical arrangements. The passages below show just a few of the planning challenges involved, including the types of intelligence that needed to be gathered and the rationalizations of personnel at the landing site. It also makes the point that it is 'essential to the rapidity and good order of the landing that congestion on the beaches should be prevented.' Congestion of humans and vehicles was indeed a problem on D-Day at many of the beaches, a product of the many variables that affect a mission once underway, plus the difficulties of properly combat-loading the waves of amphibious landing craft. During the landings, therefore, it became imperative for assault troops to clear routes off the beach for both men and armour, otherwise they would remain stuck under the sights of the German guns.

Manual of Combined Operations (1938)

CHAPTER 19
SPECIAL INTELLIGENCE REQUIRED IN CONNECTION WITH LANDINGS ON HOSTILE SHORES

1. In view of the peculiar difficulties inherent in landing hostile shore, certain detailed information is of outstanding importance in addition to that normally required in warlike operations. The special information required is that concerned with the character of possible landing places; whether they are free of defences; and if not, the type and scale of those defences.

2. Information regarding the character of possible landing places should include :—

    (i) Distance from deep water. Whether anchorages, either sheltered or open, are available for heavy, medium or light draught ships.

    (ii) Depth of water in the approaches, including the positions of rocks and shoals which may hamper landing craft—particularly shoals close off the landing places.

(iii) Other hydrographic information affecting the passage of landing craft between deep water and landing places, by day and by night. Set and rate of currents.

(iv) Slope and nature of the foreshore at various states of tide. Rise and fall of tide. Liability of landing places to be affected by bad weather.

(v) Nature of the terrain in the vicinity of the landing places. Exits from landing places. Possible advanced landing grounds for aircraft in the vicinity.

(vi) Hydrographic and topographic information affecting the employment of naval gunfire in support of the landing.

3. Information regarding beach defences should include patrol craft, mines and obstructions in the approaches, in addition to the defences on land and the probable availability of aircraft.

4. Besides that which can be derived from charts and maps, much of this information should be obtainable by peacetime reconnaissance and through secret agents both in peace and war. It may, however, be necessary to supplement this by wartime reconnaissance, either while the operation is being planned or shortly before the landing takes place.

5. Whether reconnaissance is advisable and, if so, the form it should take will depend on the value attached to surprise and the extent to which reconnaissance is liable to impair the chances of achieving it.

6. *Military reconnaissance* will seldom be feasible and unless it can be carried out with complete secrecy it will seriously endanger the chances of surprise. A detailed examination of the landing places, even if carried out by night, would, however, be of great value and the possibility of such reconnaissance should be borne in mind.

7. *Naval reconnaissance* may be either in force or by stealth. A reconnaissance in force would be of great value, particularly if it included vessels suitable for working close inshore and aircraft; but it would make any subsequent surprise very unlikely. Reconnaissance by stealth can be carried out either by submarines, small surface vessels (such as motor torpedo boats) or disguised merchant vessels or fishing craft. If there is deep water close to the landing places submarines are the most suitable vessels for this duty owing to their being able to observe while remaining virtually invisible; but when carrying out a reconnaissance submerged a submarine is handicapped by the small "height of eye" provided by a periscope.

8. *Air reconnaissance*, apart from that carried out as part of a naval reconnaissance in force, may be effected without arousing the enemy's suspicions if it can be combined with other air operations which the enemy

has no reason to suppose have any connection with landing operations. Air photographs of beaches at different states of the tide will be of value in determining the slope of the beach, a matter on which information may be important. They can also supply fair tactical information on such points as possible assembly positions, beach exits, objectives for the assaulting force including any recently constructed defences, tank obstacles, the enemy's lines of approach, etc.

[. . .]

Advanced Bases

22. For the success of a landing on a hostile shore far from the ports of embarkation the use of an advanced base or bases, either in friendly or hostile territory, may be a necessary preliminary. Such bases, including the advanced air stations which may be needed for attaining air superiority may vary in degree from temporary anchorages for hoisting out landing craft or transferring troops from transport to small war vessels, temporary fuelling bases for naval forces or temporary landing grounds for aircraft, to fully equipped defended ports and air stations. If a long sea voyage is involved and the crews of tanks, etc., are not in the same ships as their vehicles, it may also be necessary to use an advanced base to tranship the crews.

23. In the event of a landing being followed by extensive operations supplied and reinforced by landing craft working on beaches or at improvised piers, the use of an advanced base for transhipping supplies to the landing craft, for general administrative purposes and for keeping the landing craft in repair will be an important feature. Such a base may also have to include rest camps and hospital accommodation for the forces taking part in the main operation, and a repair organization for aircraft and aero engines.

24. The establishment of a fully equipped advanced base or advanced air station in an area where we do not normally exercise defensive control will in itself be a combined operation of the type considered in Part VIII of this manual, and may even include an opposed landing. The scale and form of attack against which the base must be defended will depend on geographical conditions and the disposition of enemy forces, but in general it may be said that the strategical requirements of a landing on a hostile shore call for so marked a naval superiority that attack by heavy surface forces on the base need not be considered. Conversely an advanced base will be within striking range of enemy aircraft and air defence will therefore be required on as complete a scale as practicable.

25. When considering whether and to what extent advanced bases should be used, the probable effect on surprise of establishing a base prior to the landing must be fully considered.

26. Whenever practicable the same advanced base should be used for naval, military and air purposes, both for economy in defence and for administrative efficiency.

[. . .]

CHAPTER 23
BEACH ORGANIZATION

General

1. To enable disembarkation subsequent to the landing of the first flight to be carried out efficiently, the beaches must be organized and piers and beach roadways constructed, organization and construction proceeding concurrently with the landing.

Nomenclature

2. For purposes of decentralization of control, the portion of the coast on which the landing is to take place is divided into "beaches," "sections" and "landing points."

3. The beaches will be divided into sections, so that each ship or group of ships of the same nature, discharges to a separate section. The size of a section will depend on the discharging capacity of the group of ships allotted to it, whether the ships contain troops, animals, mechanical transport or stores, and the number of landing places and exits available. Sizes of sections and the strength of beach parties will therefore vary considerably.

4. One or more landing points will be organized on each section of the beach. Landing points will be chosen according to the facilities they offer for beaching craft, landing vehicles or building piers, and their proximity to exits. Where exits are not restricted and troops and vehicles can leave the beach almost anywhere, the space for handling and discharging landing craft will be the primary consideration. The nearer the landing points are together without causing congestion, the easier will be the resumption of military control after the forces have landed.

Assembly Positions

5. On disembarkation from landing craft, troops and material landed subsequent to the first flight require to be reorganized and redistributed before military operations are undertaken. The extent to which this is necessary will depend on the type of landing craft employed and on how far it has been possible to keep units together. The extent to which it is possible will depend on the tactical situation and the progress of earlier flights. In the first place, assembly positions are chosen close to the beach, but clear of it. Subsequently, more elaborate arrangements can be made and assembly positions selected

with due regard both to their accessibility and to tactical considerations. To provide for the possibility of re-embarkation these latter positions should be within the final covering position.

6. Assembly positions will be identified by flags, or, if the landing takes place by night, by coloured lamps, but no lights will be shown without the permission of the P.M.L.O. and the concurrence of the P.B.M. (*see* paras. 18 and 19).

7. Guides, according to the size of the force, will be detailed by the M.L.Os to each assembly position for the guidance of units to that position.

Beach Roadways and Piers

8. The provision of beach roadways and piers as soon as possible after the landing of the first flight will usually be of importance. Beach roadways will probably be needed for landing guns and M.T. vehicles; and piers, either fixed or floating, will be of value in accelerating disembarkation and keeping weapons, ammunition stores, etc., dry. Provision of piers for the evacuation of wounded must also be considered.

9. Arrangements for construction of all beach roadways and piers will be made by the army. Where it is intended to employ dumb lighters or similar craft, either floating or sunk as foundations, the navy will assist in placing and securing them. The navy may also be able to provide suitable craft for the purpose at the request of the army. A list of the principal factors affecting the provision of piers is given in Appendix XVI.

Marking of Beaches and Sections

10. The beaches will be lettered from right to left facing inland.

11. The sections will be numbered from right to left facing inland and each section will be known by the letter of the beach of which it is a subdivision, followed by the section number. Thus, "A" beach might have three sections, A1, A2, A3.

12. The limits of sections will be marked by coloured discs by day and by lamps of corresponding colour by night. In the centre of each section will be placed a notice board bearing the distinguishing letter and number of the section, which must be visible at a distance of 400 yards, both from the sea and land sides.

13. To enable troops to clear the landing points as quickly possible, sufficient signposts should be provided to show the way to the assembly positions.

Line of Demarcation between Naval and Military Responsibility on Beaches

14. The line of demarcation between the areas of naval and military responsibility is the landward edge of that area which it is necessary to keep

clear in order to enable the discharge of landing craft to proceed without delay. The distance of this line from the water's edge necessarily depends on local conditions, but this distance should be decided previous to the landing by the Principal Beach Master and Principal Military Landing Officer in collaboration.

15. The navy is responsible for the landing of troops, animals, vehicles and stores, and will control the beach and the land adjacent to it up to the line of demarcation.

16. Within this area the beach masters are responsible for clearing the landing craft, passing troops across to their assembly positions, and taking vehicles, guns, stores, etc., to the dumps on the line of demarcation (*see* para. 29).

17. Everything inshore of the line of demarcation comes under military control. The military area may or may not include the initial assembly positions, but will include the later assembly positions, military dumps and loading-up places for land transport.

Control of Beaches

18. *Principal Beach Master (P.B.M.).*—A naval officer of senior rank will at the outset be appointed as P.B.M. He will be responsible to the S.N.O.L. and will have control of all landing craft on the beaches and of all personnel and material within the naval area. He should work in close co-operation with the military authorities ashore, and in this he will be assisted by the Principal Military Landing Officer. His main object will be to ensure the most rapid discharge and "turn round" of all landing craft consistent with meeting military requirements.

19. *Principal Military Landing Officer (P.M.L.O.).*—The P.M.L.O. is an officer of the O.M.G.'s branch of the staff. Within the area of naval control he collaborates with the P.B.M., whom it is his duty to assist in co-ordinating the work of the navy and army on the beaches. He is responsible for clearing the dumps on the line of demarcation. Inshore of this area he should supervise the arrangements for guiding troops to the assembly positions.

20. *Beach Master (B.M.).*—A naval officer is appointed as B.M. for each beach. He is responsible to the P.B.M. for the rapid and safe clearing and "turn round" of the landing craft at his beach. He should obtain from the Military Landing Officer the necessary personnel required to clear the landing craft and beach of men and material. He is responsible that the beach signal station gets into communication with the ships discharging on to his beach and with the nearest military signal station inshore. If sufficient motor boats are available one in charge of a naval officer should be allotted to work under the orders of each B.M. for directing the movements of landing craft and taking lines ashore.

21. *Military Landing Officer (M.L.O.)*.—A M.L.O. is appointed to assist each B.M. He obtains and organizes the military beach parties required by the B.M. and arranges for their meals and reliefs. His duties include assisting the B.M. in forwarding men to the assembly positions, transferring stores to the military dumps (*see* para. 38), ensuring the maintenance of signal communication inshore, and controlling the exits from the beach. Should military working parties be required in addition to those detailed, the M.L.O. should make arrangements to obtain them.

22. *Assistant Beach Master (A.B.M.)*.—A naval Officer appointed as A.B.M. for each section of the beach. He is responsible to the B.M. for the beaching, discharge and turn round of the landing craft on his section of the beach. With the assistance of the Assistant Military Landing Officer he should distribute and control the naval and military beach parties told off for the section.

23. *Assistant Military Landing Officer (A.M.L.O.)*.—The A.M.L.O. assists the M.L.O. and A.B.M.

24. *Beach Lieutenant, R.N.*—A Beach Lieutenant is appointed for each landing point. He is responsible to the A.B.M. for control of landing craft and naval and military beach parties at his landing point.

25. *Royal Air Force Landing Officer (R.A.F.L.O.)*.—R.A.F.L.Os. may in certain circumstances be appointed in lieu of M.L.Os., when they will carry out similar duties to those laid down for the M.L.Os.

[. . .]

It is important that the P.B.M. and all the beach staff should work in close touch with the P.S.T.O. and transport staff.

Duties of Beach Personnel

27. The first stage of a landing likely to meet with opposition may have to be carried out under very trying conditions for the parties working on the beaches. These parties should consist of personnel under naval and military discipline. Their first duties on landing will be to mark out the beaches, sections, landing points, exits, assembly positions, sites for dumps, etc., in readiness for landing the remainder of the assaulting force and any subsequent forces and supplies.

28. Naval beach parties must be detailed for each landing point. Their particular work is that of beaching or securing landing craft, assisting the crews to haul off when unloaded, and generally performing the duties for which a knowledge of seamanship is required.

29. Although the work of unloading the landing craft is under naval control and the handling of the craft will require the services of naval ratings,

it is improbable that sufficient naval personnel will be available for unloading and transporting stores, etc., up the beach. Military or air force working parties must, therefore, be detailed to work on the beaches under the beach masters to clear the landing craft and transfer stores, etc., to the dumps on the line of demarcation (*see* para. 16). Other parties for clearing these dumps will be organized separately under the control of the P.M.L.O. There must, however, be close co-operation between the P.B.M. and the P.M.L.O. in this as in other matters to ensure that the proportion of available labour allocated to the respective areas is adjusted according to the progress of the disembarkation.

Strength of Beach Parties

30. It is not possible to lay down exactly the strength of the various working parties which will be required. The strength of naval parties will depend on the size and number of the landing craft, whether they are self-propelled or not, and the nature of the beach. That of military or air force parties will depend on the size and number of the landing craft, the distance that stores, etc., have to be transported, the nature of the loads, the types of piers and roadways and the facilities for lifting weights. The matter is one calling for the judgment of officers of all Services with practical experience, and the organization must be sufficiently elastic to meet unexpected or changing conditions.

31. Working parties must be detailed initially to beach sections and landing points, but, as the landing progresses and piers are built the number of landing points will decrease. The parties can then be reorganized into reliefs.
[. . .]

Clearing of Beaches

37. It is essential to the rapidity and good order of the landing that congestion on the beaches should be prevented. All troops must clear the landing points immediately and make straight for the assembly positions. No accumulation of stores or material near the water's edge should be allowed. Vehicles should be moved away as soon as landed. In order to enable this to be done with horse-drawn vehicles, horses should be landed with their harness on and at the same time as the vehicles. Vehicles should never be landed before the unit to which they belong. Mechanical aids such as winches, capstans, tackles, ropeways for cliffs, tractors, etc., should be employed if circumstances permit.

CHAPTER 2

NAVAL AND AIR SUPPORT

The two major factors working in the Allies' favour on D-Day were its undoubted superiority in naval and in air forces. The total Allied naval forces used for the operation included 1,213 warships, 4,126 landing craft, 736 ancillary craft and 864 merchant vessels. By contrast, the potential threat from the Kriegsmarine (German Navy) in the area of operations was little more than 100 relatively minor surface vessels, mostly E-boats, R-boats and minesweepers, with a handful of U-boats projecting power from the Atlantic ports. In fact, the greatest threat to the Operation *Neptune* fleet actually came from naval mines and coastal guns, which claimed 37 vessels on 6 June, most of the victims small landing craft types destroyed as they approached the enemy coastline. Casualties could have been far worse, however. Much of the German coastal firepower was suppressed by Allied bombing raids and naval preparatory gunfire, while the mine threat was mitigated by some 350 minesweeping vessels, which worked relentlessly on 5–6 June clearing invasion routes of as many mines as possible.

Another potential threat to the Allied armada came from the Luftwaffe, which since 1940 had made the seas between Britain and continental Europe perilous territory to traverse. Yet the combined strength of the US Army Air Forces (USAAF) and the Royal Air Force (RAF) was beyond challenge. On 6 June, the air operations around and beyond the beachheads were supported by some 9,500 Allied aircraft, including 7,000 fighters and tactical strike aircraft and 2,000 medium and heavy bombers. This aerial onslaught was initially resisted by just 319 operational aircraft of the German Third Air Fleet, meaning that the Allies snatched air superiority immediately, a status that they maintained over the subsequent weeks despite the Luftwaffe's injection of another 1,000 aircraft into the theatre.

The first extract below is from the US Navy manual *Landing Operations Doctrine* (FTP 167). The very brief introduction, written by Admiral H. R. Stark, explains that 'FTP-167 is intended as a guide for forces of the Navy and Marine Corps conducting a landing against opposition. It considers, primarily, the tactics and technique of the landing operation and the necessary supporting measures therefore.' In the passage given here, the focus is on explaining the principles of naval supporting gunfire, which on D-Day delivered a critical 40-minute initial bombardment as landing forces approached the beach areas, and later gave further support as the Allied troops attempted to advance inland. In just 10 minutes alone, warships fired 2,000 tons of shells, in a spectacle never forgotten by those who witnessed it.

Landing Operations Doctrine (1938)

Chapter V
NAVAL GUNFIRE
Section I

MISSION

501. Naval gunfire mission.—In amphibious operations, it is the mission of certain naval task groups to replace the landing force artillery in supporting the assaulting troops by fire on shore targets. That is, by delivering fire on enemy personnel, weapons, and other defensive installations, and on critical terrain features which may conceal undiscovered enemy positions, ship batteries enable the landing force first to land, then to advance, hold, or withdraw, with fewer casualties than would otherwise be possible. In some cases, effective naval gunfire may be the critical factor which determines success or failure.

502. Characteristics of defensive positions.—

a. The exact nature of the fires required in the fulfillment of the above missions depends on the character of the defense against which the amphibious attack is launched. In the absence of definite information to the contrary, it must always be assumed that the assault will be met by an organized defense, and a suitable fire plan must be executed based on this assumption with probable targets located by a study of the terrain.

b. The defense of an area on which a beachhead is to be established will comprise naval, air, and ground forces. All of these defenses must be engaged and rendered ineffective prior to and during the assault to an extent that will permit the establishment of the landing force ashore. Naval gunfire will have an obvious role in the engagement of air and naval defense forces, but provision must be made for these actions, separate from the fire power allotted to the engagement of the ground defense with which this chapter is concerned.

c. The character of the defense which will be met in any one instance will depend on:

1. The terrain.

      2. The tactical doctrine of the enemy.

      3. The size, composition, and morale of the enemy force.

All of these factors must be carefully considered on the basis of available information, and the gunfire plan fitted to the estimate of each situation.

    d. However, regardless of terrain, enemy doctrine, and the local enemy force, the ground defense may be considered in the following categories:

      1. The beach defenses.

      2. Tactical defense areas inland (strong points).

      3. Artillery.

      4. Observation and command posts, communication nets, supply areas.

      5. Reserves.

[. . .]

    e. *Beach Defenses.* —This term is taken to include both passive and active weapons, which are installed on or in the immediate vicinity of the landing area, and the troops which man the weapons. Passive weapons are such installations as land mines, barbed wire, and other obstacles. The active weapons are principally machine guns and light, rapid-fire artillery pieces, emplaced to deliver direct fire on the beaches and the immediate sea approaches. The number of these weapons and the size of the forces manning them will vary with each situation, and their actual locations will rarely be definitely known in advance. But in all cases heavy fire must be maintained on their known or probable positions during the approach of the assault landing waves to the beach.

    f. *Strongpoints.*—The terrain inland from the beach will contain a varying number of localities which lend themselves to defensive organization (hills, ridges, stream lines, villages, etc.). These localities are also normally the critical areas which the landing force must seize to secure the beachhead. These strongpoints may or may not be occupied by enemy troops and if occupied the strength of the defensive unit may vary from a squad to a battalion. However, those strongpoints immediately in rear and to the flanks of the landing beaches must be engaged by fire prior to the landing of the assault waves and fire power must be immediately available to engage these strongpoints, and others further inland, when it is found necessary by the attacking troops.

g. *Artillery.*—Any active defense of an area suitable for landing operations will normally be supported by both field artillery and coast artillery batteries.

    1. The coast artillery normally has a mission to deny the use of the sea approaches. These batteries are permanent installations and must be rendered ineffective before or during the debarkation period. If there is any likelihood of a coast battery being still in firing condition on D-day, its engagement must be planned for by the assignment of one of the largest naval batteries available to this task.

    2. Field artillery is mobile and can move rapidly from place to place in the accomplishment of its mission to place fire on the attacking troops. The location of field artillery batteries will rarely be known prior to the attack, but from a study of the terrain, positions suitable for batteries can be determined and fires should be planned for these areas. Naval gunfire must be prepared to place fire immediately on field artillery batteries discovered in position whether or not they are actually firing.

h. *Observation and command posts, communication nets, supply areas.* —These are secondary targets and they should be engaged only if definitely located and if ammunition is available above the requirements of more immediately important targets.

    1. The defense depends on ground as well as air observers for vital information as to the nature, strength, and point of attack in order that troops may be alerted and disposed to meet the attack, and in order that mortar and field artillery fire may be adjusted on the attackers. These observation posts will normally be on high ground both in the beach area and further inland, usually within the perimeter of a strongpoint. Naval gunfire may blind the enemy during the debarkation and beach assault periods by engagement of areas containing these observation posts.

    2. The commanders of defending units will establish command posts in small areas centrally located with respect to the various defensive installations. These command posts are normally in defilade and under cover from air observation and consequently will rarely be definitely located. If, however, their positions are known, fire may be placed on the areas in order to disrupt the execution of the defensive plan.

    3. The defense depends on its communications (wire, radio, roads) for transmission of information, orders, troops and supplies. Fires should be planned for critical points in the

communication net in order that they may be delivered on call if schedule fires on these points are not practicable. The critical points are the command posts (since in their vicinity are usually located switchboards and radio sets), and road junctions, bridges, fords, and other restricted points in the road system whose destruction or blocking will impede the mobility of the defenders.

4. Supplies represented by ammunition dumps, oil storage areas, truck parks, etc., are remunerative targets for naval gunfire if located. They will normally be of easy access to roads or trails, and in the absence of suitable personnel or weapon targets probable supply dump areas should be engaged.

i. *Reserves.*—Regardless of the number of troops committed to the defense by occupation of the beach positions and of the strongpoints immediately in rear of the beaches, a good proportion of the defense forces will normally be held in reserve in centrally located areas.

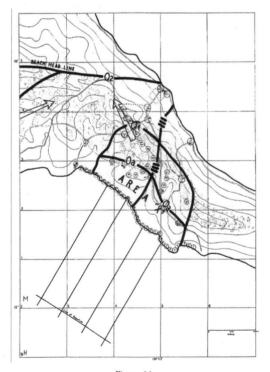

Figure 11.

Bivouac areas of these units should be engaged early in the naval gunfire plan and provision must always be made to bring heavy fire to bear immediately on these reserves moving up to meet the attack.

j. Figure 11 indicates a possible organization for defense by the trace of targets. But it must be clearly understood that definite information on targets will be meager prior to the attack, that enemy tactics and doctrine will vary. In the absence of specific information the principle must be followed of placing fire at the proper times in all areas from which, should he be there, the enemy could defeat the attack.

503. Relative Importance of Targets.—The relative importance of the targets which naval gunfire must engage will vary according to the stage of the attack. During the debarkation period, active coast batteries are the most important, with known beach defenses and other definitely located troops next in order. During the ship to shore movement of assault boat waves, the beach defense areas and the strongpoint areas commanding the beaches are the priority targets. These areas must be covered completely during this period. Fire must also be maintained on any coast batteries still active and on active field artillery batteries. If any ship batteries remain unemployed, and if the ammunition supply permits, other targets of importance which should be engaged during this phase are definitely located enemy reserves and rear area strongpoints known to be occupied. During the period of the attack inland most of the targets will be designated by personnel ashore with the landing force. Any target so designated should take precedence over targets designated by other means. Of targets designated by the landing force (or by air observers), a counterattack is of primary importance, with enemy weapons such as artillery, mortars or machine guns next.

504. Classification of fires.—The fires executed in the general performance of the naval gunfire mission may be classified as follows:

a. *Effect sought:*

1. Neutralization.

2. Destruction.

b. *Form:*

1. Concentrations.

2. Point fires.

c. *Prearrangement:*

1. Fires delivered on time schedule.

2. Fires delivered on call.

3. Fires on targets of opportunity.

d. *Tactical purpose:*

1. Preparation.

2. Close support.

3. Deep support.

4. Special missions.

e. *Method of fire control:*

1. Direct fire.

2. Indirect fire.

Definitions.–

a. *Effect sought.*—

1. *Neutralization.*—Neutralization fire is area fire delivered for the purpose of causing severe losses, hampering or interrupting movement or action and, in general, to destroy the combat efficiency of enemy personnel. In the usual case, neutralization is only temporary and the target becomes active soon after fire ceases. Neutralization is accomplished by short bursts of fire of great density to secure the advantage and effect of shock and surprise. Most targets engaged by naval gunfire will be of the type for which neutralization is appropriate.

2. *Destruction*—The term is applied to fire delivered for the express purpose of destruction and when it is reasonable to expect that relatively complete destruction can be attained. Destruction should be attempted only under favorable conditions of target designation and observation.

b. *Form.–*

1. *Concentrations.*—A concentration is a volume of fire placed on an area within a limited time. It is the form used for neutralization. The term is applicable regardless of the tactical purpose of the fire. Concentrations may be plotted in the form of numbered circles with the principal part of the target at the center of the circle.

2. *Point fires.*—Point fire is fire directed at a definite material target to destroy that particular object. Point fires may also be plotted by a numbered circle, usually of smaller size than those used for plotting concentrations.

c. *Prearrangement.*—

1. *Fires delivered on time schedule.*—Some schedule fires can be definitely planned in advance, both as to time and as to place. A time schedule is made for the purpose of coordinating these fires with the movement of the assault boat waves or with the advance

of attacking troops on shore. This schedule may be in tabular or graphic form. The time will normally be shown as so many minutes before or after (minus or plus) H-hour, in order that the actual clock time of execution of these fires may be changed by simply changing the time of H-hour. This principle of flexibility is especially applicable to the preparation. The time schedule fires in this Phase must conform closely to the actual movement of the assault boat waves at each beach.

2. *Fires delivered on call.*—These are fires which are planned in advance as to location but which are delivered only upon request. They are plotted in the form of numbered concentrations for ease in designating them when required.

3. *Fires on targets on opportunity.*—Targets of opportunity are targets which appear to the observer and which have not been plotted for execution on time schedule or on call. Observers may designate these targets to the firing ships by reference to a plotted concentration, by coordinates from a grid system standardized for the operation, or by other means.

d. *Tactical purpose.*—

1. *Preparation.*—This term is used to designate intensive fire delivered on the landing beaches and adjacent areas during the approach to the beach of the landing craft of the leading wave.

2. *Close support.*—This term designates those fires furnished in support of units ashore. It is fire placed on enemy troops, weapons, or positions which, because of their proximity, present the most immediate and serious threat to the supported unit.

3. *Deep support.*—This term includes the more distant fires furnished in support of the operation as a whole as distinguished from those of direct and immediate benefit to front line troops. Characteristic applications are fires placed on enemy artillery, on enemy reserves, and on critical points or areas which it is desired to prevent the enemy from using.

4. *Special missions.*—These may be considered as a type of deep supporting fire for which large caliber naval guns are particularly suitable, such as long range fire on cities, airfields and seacoast batteries, and the destruction of heavy permanent fortifications.

e. *Method of fire control.*—

1. *Direct fire.*—Direct fires are fires delivered on targets which can be seen from the firing ship. Spotting of the fall of shot is normally carried out from the ship.

USS *Arkansas* (BB-33) fires her 12in guns at German positions, off Omaha Beach on 6 June 1944.

2. *Indirect fire.*—Indirect fires are fires delivered on targets which cannot be seen from the ship. These fires are spotted by plane spotters or by spotters on shore.

Landing Operations on Hostile Shores was published in June 1941, only months prior to the American entry into the war. Its key purpose was to present doctrine related to 'The securing of a beachhead from which to project major land operations', and to do so from a joint forces perspective. In its Chapter 7, it addresses the crucial topic of coordinating a landing operation with an air campaign, making the point that 'local air superiority is essential to the success of a landing operation', as indeed would be proved on D-Day. The air operations that day were diverse in type. On the night of 5–6 June, for example, RAF Short Stirling bombers from 218 (Gold Coast) Squadron dropped tons of metal 'chaff' strips between Dover and Calais to confuse German coastal radar operators. US B-26 Marauder bombers laid smoke screens across the Normandy coastline as the Allied fleet approached. Heavy bombers pounded the coastal fortifications and other major logistical and military targets, while Allied Forward Air Controllers (FACs) with the ground units could radio in strikes from waiting P-47 Thunderbolts or Hawker Typhoons. The product was a uniquely hostile environment for German ground troops.

Landing Operations on Hostile Shores (1941)

Chapter 7   Aviation
Section I   General

[. . .]

177. Air Superiority.—

    a. Whether or not an advance air base has been secured, local air superiority is essential to the success of a landing operation. Troop transports and troops in small boats offer concentrated targets for hostile aircraft and are extremely vulnerable to bombing and gas attacks. Even a small opposing air force skillfully handled and not effectively neutralized may disrupt the landing and force a withdrawal. It is therefore essential that hostile combat aviation capable of intervening during the landing operations be destroyed or neutralized prior to the approach of the transports and supporting naval units within the transport area. Subsequently, supporting aviation must be prepared to furnish protection against air attacks during the critical landing phase.

    b. Operations to neutralize the defending air forces include destruction of airdromes and planes on the ground and aerial combat. The enemy will, if possible, utilize a large number of landing fields, camouflage will be employed to the maximum to protect his establishments, and dummy planes will be displayed, actual planes being widely separated and camouflaged. Thus, thorough reconnaissance is necessary before successful attacks can be launched. To render enemy landing fields unusable requires extensive operations and a heavy expenditure of bombs.

178. Air Support.—

    a. Responsibility for air support and for control of the air within the zone of the proposed operation usually rests initially with the naval aviation of the attack force until such time as adequate support is practicable by land-based aviation of the landing force. Any available aircraft of the landing force participates. Naval aviation is relieved progressively by aircraft of the landing force as soon as facilities for their operation can be provided.

    b. Pilots, observers, and other aviation personnel of the Army may be utilized by the Navy when naval planes are engaged in land reconnaissance, attack in support of ground operations, and similar missions. When this is envisaged, it must be appreciated that special training of Army personnel will be necessary because of differences in naval types of aircraft and in naval procedure.

    c. The closest cooperation is required between air units, the supported troops, and the naval fire support group.

179. Composition of Air Force.—In general, the circumstances affecting the composition of the air force lie between the following two extremes: the most favorable situation, which is that permitting employment of all types of Army aviation from adequate, well-located land bases throughout the operation; and the most disadvantageous situation, which makes necessary the employment of naval aviation alone in support of the landing and the initial advance. in any situation, however, the air force should be composed of the classes of aviation which can best accomplish the following missions:

First, gain and maintain local air superiority.

Second, close support the landing force.

Third, furnish necessary reconnaissance and observation, including photographic missions.

180. Air Reconnaissance.—Information regarding the hostile defenses, and the number and suitability of landing beaches and approaches thereto may prove more essential to the success of the landing than benefits derived from attempted surprise without this knowledge. Strategical surprise against an alert enemy is exceedingly difficult to obtain. Air and surface scouting by enemy air forces will probably result in early discovery of the approaching expedition. While it is seldom possible to conduct intensive distant aerial reconnaissance without sacrifice of strategical surprise, it is often feasible to include aerial reconnaissance missions among the general air operations being carried out in the theater in such manner that the enemy will be unable to derive any definite conclusions therefrom. Prior to the landing, tactical reconnaissance of beaches and contiguous areas inland is conducted over a broad front, and concentration of air activities over the particular sectors where landings are planned is carefully avoided. Marked aerial activity over several areas may, in fact, be used as a demonstration or a feint and thereby aid in gaining tactical surprise. Because of the ability of air missions to cover extensive areas or numerous beaches, aerial reconnaissance and photography provided satisfactory means of obtaining general information without sacrificing tactical surprise.

181. Transportation of Aircraft.—

    a. Because a landing requires the maximum employment of available aviation, every effort is made to provide for the early participation of Army aircraft. Where aircraft can fly the entire distance from their home base to the scene of the landing, or where advance air bases have been secured, few serious problems are involved.

    b. When land bases are lacking, carriers may be assigned for use of the landing force aircraft; failing this, the airplanes may be assigned to the fleet carriers. If carrier space does not permit the adoption of either of these plans, the airplanes may be stowed aboard carriers for initial launching only. Another plan is to carry airplanes fully set up on auxiliary vessels, launching to be effected by catapulting or from specially constructed take-off platform. A less desirable alternative is to use transports which permit airplanes to be stowed above and below decks partially set up. These airplanes can be transferred to carriers for final assembly and launching. Least desirable is the method of transporting airplanes knocked down and crated. Crated aircraft are cumbersome, difficult to put into operation, and cannot be made ready for use until al considerable beachhead or advance air base has been gained.

Section II
Air Operations Preliminary to Landing

    182. Reconnaissance.—Aerial reconnaissance is made when the necessity for information of terrain, hydrographic conditions, enemy defensive measures, and suitability of beaches outweighs considerations of surprise. When aerial reconnaissance is made, it is so conducted that it will serve to confuse the hostile defenders as to the probable points of landing. Air reconnaissance by troop commanders is desirable.

    183. Photography.—

    a. Air photographs and mosaics, carefully studied, are of assistance in drawing up final plans for the operation. Airplanes flying at high altitudes are able under favorable conditions to obtain the required data without sacrificing tactical surprise.

b. Air photographs are particularly useful in determining the best channels of approach to beaches, the location and character of defensive works and installations, presence of obstacles, the configuration of the ground at the beaches, and the amount of surf to be encountered. Some indication of depth of water and underwater obstructions is also gained by comparing views taken at low and high tides.

c. Oblique photographs, particularly those taken from seaward, are valuable to boat group officers in identifying beaches, to troop commanders in planning operations on shore, and to gunnery officers in selecting targets and aiming points and planning the gunfire support.

184. Reduction of Hostile Defenses.—Prior to landing, unless secrecy is the primary consideration, advantage must be taken of every opportunity to deliver air attacks on the hostile defenses. Aircraft, airdromes, aviation matériel, fortifications, gun emplacements, communication and transportation centers, supply bases, and troop movements and concentrations are appropriate targets.

Section III
Air Operations During Debarkation

185. Protection of Transport Area.—

a. Protection is furnished to the vessels of the attack force during debarkation into small boats by denying hostile aviation access to the landing area. Neutralization is obtained by the use of pursuit aviation and the coordinated support of the antiaircraft defenses, and by attacking hostile aircraft on the ground.

b. Submarines are an additional menace during debarkation. Employment of scouting planes equipped with bombs for attacking submarines reduces this hazard. Battleship and cruiser aircraft not required for gunnery observation are also employed to establish an air patrol.

c. In planning the time of arrival in the transport area, consideration is given to the disadvantages of operating aircraft during darkness. It is extremely difficult to provide proper air support for a night landing in the presence of an alert hostile air force because the transport area can be illuminated by flares and effectively bombed by the defenders.

186. Reconnaissance.—Intensive and continuous reconnaissance of hostile defenses and shore establishments is initiated prior to or simultaneously with the debarkation, or as soon thereafter as visibility permits. Beach defenses, artillery positions, airdromes, and the locations of enemy general reserves are reconnoitered intensively. Definite knowledge of the enemy dispositions gained at this time will exercise a material effect on the later employment of aviation.

187. **Attacks on Shore Objectives.**—During debarkation of leading landing groups some aircraft may supplement naval gunfire on the beach defenses while others are utilized against airdromes and any movement of enemy reserves.

The British *Manual of Combined Operations* also thoroughly acknowledged the support requirements for a successful amphibious landing operation. In addition, in the passage here it reflects on the use of warships and transport vessels in the combat, and also the need to achieve as much concealment as possible on the approach to the hostile shore. For the D-Day landings, the option of night landings was rejected outright, although much of the approach transit was conducted under the cover of darkness. The sheer scale of the *Neptune* operation (in some cases it took nearly nine hours for ships to get into their correct disembarkation positions), plus challenges such as coastal navigation, gunfire coordination and negotiating beach obstacles, meant that the landings had to go in at daybreak to optimise the chances of success.

Manual of Combined Operations (1938)

CHAPTER 20
STRATEGICAL REQUIREMENTS AND PRELIMINARY OPERATIONS

Naval Requirements

1. The main function required of naval strategy in connection with landings on hostile shores is to guard against interference by enemy naval forces. This requirement, common to all oversea expeditions, is of an unusually exacting order in the case of landing operations in view of the fact that the transports and some of the warships engaged are immobilized close to an enemy coast and lose that freedom of movement which is an important asset in most naval operations. It follows that, except in the case of a surprise operation needing only a few hours for its completion, a considerable superiority of naval force in the area of operations is essential.

2. Protection from the enemy's main forces will as a rule be provided by the operations of our battlefleet, possibly at a great distance from, and having little direct connection with, the landing operations. But battlefleet cover cannot ensure complete protection against surface ships and is of no effect against submarines and aircraft. Naval forces are therefore required as an integral part of the expedition. Should an incursion by enemy surface forces be probable, it will be advisable for a sufficient strength of the protective forces to retain their freedom of movement by acting, or being prepared to act, as a covering squadron rather than as a close escort. Under some conditions it may be advisable for this covering squadron to engage in offensive operations designed to draw off the attention of the enemy's naval forces from the landing.

3. Protection against air attack (as far as this can be supplied by naval forces) and against submarines will be provided by forces employed in more purely defensive roles close to transport landing craft.

4. Warships and transports engaged in landing operations must also be protected against mines. In addition to the use of protector paravanes, extensive minesweeping will usually be required.

Air Requirements

5. The comparatively easy targets presented by ships anchored or restricted in their movements off an enemy coast, and the virtual defencelessness of land forces in landing craft and during disembarkation, render a force engaged in a landing on a hostile shore particularly susceptible to air attack. The main aim of air strategy in this connection is therefore to assert the superiority of our air forces over those of the enemy so decisively as to prohibit any sustained attack on the expedition, either while it is approaching the coast or during the landing operations.

6. The method of achieving this aim will depend upon whether the enterprise can be covered by the general operations of our air forces or not. If the landing is to be effected in an area which is covered by the operations of air forces already in the theatre and in enjoyment of a general ascendency over the air forces opposed to them, the method will usually be to intensify air operations against all enemy air forces within striking range of the scene of the proposed landing to such an extent that they will be impotent to interfere effectively. On the other hand, the landing may be planned to take place in an area at a distance from that covered by the main air operations and the enemy may have unneutralized air forces within striking range of that area. Under these conditions it will be necessary to undertake special air operations, and by establishing the ascendency of our own air forces in the area, render the enemy air forces ineffective.

7. The scope of the operations necessary to establish the ascendency of our air forces in the vicinity of the landing will require careful consideration during the drawing up of the general plan of the enterprise. As the landing will be in the enemy's territory he will presumably have greater facilities for operating aircraft in the vicinity than we shall, unless it happens that we also have territory close at hand. If his forces are on a small scale this disadvantage may be overcome by the use of carrier-borne aircraft, despite the handicaps suffered by the latter both in performance and in method of operation.

8. In other circumstances, however, it may be necessary to work for air superiority from advanced air stations established in the vicinity as an essential preliminary to the main landing operations. Advanced air stations may be either for land-planes or seaplanes or both. Units operating from them may be required to work on modified scales of equipment and transport. Both sea and air transport may be employed in equipping them, and the aircraft working from them may either be flown there or transported by sea.

9. It is, however, inherent in the conditions of air warfare that the cover provided by our air force in this way can never be complete enough to guarantee entire immunity from air attack. The employment of some aircraft in a close defence rôle will, therefore, be required during the landing operations. Their operations must be considered in conjunction with the other tactical requirements of that phase.

10. Whether air superiority should be established by operations (from existing aerodromes, carriers or advanced air stations) prior to the landing, or whether no action should be taken until the seaborne forces are approaching the enemy coast, depends in first instance on the extent to which strategical surprise is liable to be sacrificed by engaging in preliminary air operations. If these operations would prejudice surprise, the advantages of surprise must be weighed against the greater degree of air superiority that prior air action will attain. Strategic surprise will, however itself assist in achieving local air superiority though it will necessarily be less effective in this respect than in overcoming the opposition land forces. Once the attack has been discovered, air forces can be brought to the area of operations so much more quickly than land forces that the effect of surprise will be soon outworn. But despite this, surprise may enable a first footing to be gained ashore before air opposition can be brought to bear.

11. Another important consideration will be to prevent enemy reconnaissance sighting the ships of the expedition, particularly during

The P-47 Thunderbolt was a resilient, powerful and well-armed ground-attack aircraft, much used over Normandy.

the last 24 hours of the approach. Not only will such a discovery of the expedition gravely prejudice the attainment of a reasonable measure of tactical surprise, but it opens the way for such air attack on the ships as the enemy may be able to muster despite the operations that have been taken to neutralize his air force. General air superiority will do much to hamper the enemy's power of reconnaissance, but, as in the case of air attack, it cannot guarantee that enemy reconnaissance aircraft will never come within sighting distance of the expedition. When therefore the expedition is within range of enemy air reconnaissance it may be necessary to employ fighter aircraft, with a view to driving off reconnoitring aircraft. The requisite aircraft will be controlled by the Naval Commander, and will usually be found by the Fleet Air Arm.

CHAPTER 21
THE APPROACH

General Considerations

1. The main considerations governing the conduct of an expedition during the period immediately prior to arrival off the landing places are:—

> (i) Whether the forces are to remain in transports until they embark in landing craft, or whether they will be transferred to warships for the final approach.

> (ii) The extent to which the approach is to be covered by darkness.

2. These matters will be considered primarily from the point of view of the assaulting force. The conduct of forces arriving subsequently will be governed by similar considerations but, as the assaulting force may by that time have made its presence known, such extensive measures for concealment may not be required.

Relative Advantages of Transports and Warships

3. The advantages of employing transports for the final approach are:—

> (i) Organization of the operation is simple.

> (ii) The troops can be given good opportunities for rest during the period immediately prior to the assault.

> (iii) All the tanks, guns and M.T. of the force are brought to the scene of operations at the same time. (Warships will not usually carry tanks, so, if warships are employed, the tanks required for the initial landing must be already in the landing craft, which would be in tow of the warships. The number of tanks immediately available would therefore be limited to the number that can be carried by the landing craft in one trip.)

4. Against the above advantages, there are some disadvantages which can be largely overcome by effecting the approach in warships. These are:—

    (i) The difficulties of manoeuvring a body of transports close to the enemy coast will be considerable, particularly if the approach is by night and if intricate navigation is required.

   (ii) If the enemy sights transports he will surmise the aim of the operations more readily than if he sights warships.

  (iii) Time will be required after arrival at the anchorage (or position from which the landing craft are to leave the ships) for hoisting out landing craft-whereas, if wars are used, the larger types of landing craft will already be in tow of the ships carrying the troops. This lapse will tend to prejudice surprise. It will also be difficult to carry out these operations quietly, and at night this may lead to detection.

Transfer of Forces from Transports to Warships

5. If warships are employed in carrying troops during the final approach of a force previously carried in transports, arrangements must be made not only for transferring the troops from transports to warships but also for hoisting out landing craft carried in the transports, together with the tanks required for the first assault. The landing craft will then have to be taken in tow by warships. This will involve either the existence of sheltered waters in a vicinity suitable for the transfer, or reliance on suitable weather conditions. If the transfer takes place by day special measures for protection from air and submarine attack will also be required.

Modifications when the Sea Passage from Base to Landing Places is Short

6. In exceptional circumstances transfer from transports to warships may take place at a base (either a special advanced base or an established base in friendly territory) within, say, a day, a night's steaming of the landing places. Alternatively the enterprise may start from such a base without any previous voyage. Under these conditions the advantages of employing warships, particularly in conjunction with landing craft specially designed for the operation, are considerably greater than in the more general cases considered below.

Concealment

7. To attain the maximum degree of surprise it will be necessary to effect as much as possible of the approach by night. From the point of view of the approach alone, the ideal is to arrive off the landing places at dawn, thus ensuring that the forces are as far as possible from the landing places at nightfall on the previous day. The requirement may, however, be modified by:—

(i) Navigational difficulties which make it inadvisable to effect the last part of the approach in darkness. In these circumstances the expedition will be still further away at the previous nightfall, but surprise immediately prior to the landing will be sacrificed.

(ii) The requirements of a night landing which may call for approach to be completed comparatively early in the night.

8. To make full use of whatever period of darkness is included in the approach it will be necessary to—

(i) Steam at as high a speed as possible during this period.

(ii) Take steps to counter the enemy's air and naval reconnaissance—

(*a*) before nightfall,

(*b*) during the night,

(*c*) when the last part of the approach is made in daylight, during that period.

9. Steps taken to counter enemy reconnaissance before nightfall will include steering deceptive courses, and stationing screens of warships and aircraft to drive off enemy surface vessels, submarines and aircraft which might otherwise sight the expedition.

10. During the night, concealment is most likely to be effected by concentrating our forces in as small an area as possible; but it may also be advisable to station warships in the positions best calculated to drive off any vessels which have sighted the expedition and are attempting to shadow it.

11. To avoid being sighted by night it is of great importance to cut down funnel smoke to a minimum. Smoke is frequently visible at much greater distances than the ship making it, and it may be the first thing to draw the attention of the enemy to the expedition.

12. When ships arriving off an enemy coast at night are required to anchor, special precautions will be required to ensure silence. When practicable, anchors should be veered down instead of let go.

13. When the last part of the approach is made in daylight, little concealment will be possible, but operations to drive off enemy reconnaissance vessels and aircraft may still be of some value.

Navigational Considerations

14. The navigational requirements of the approach will depend on the number and type of ships taking part and on the situation of the anchorage or position from which the landing craft will leave the ships for the assault on the beaches. Decisions regarding this position, and whether or not ships will anchor, will depend mainly on the choice of the landing places and the method of carrying out the assault. These matters are included in the next chapter but

they will have to be considered in conjunction with the navigational problems involved in the approach.

15. When the last part of the approach is made at night, special navigational aids may be needed. Light buoys could probably be placed in prearranged positions by submarines, M.T.Bs or other small vessels shortly before the arrival of the expedition; or lights could be shown from these vessels themselves station required positions. In the latter case it could be arranged to keep the lights screened from shoreward. The advantage of employing submarines for this duty is that they can approach the enemy coast unseen during the previous day, and, except off low-lying coasts, can fix their positions accurately through their periscopes before dark.

16. The use of Taut Wire Measuring Gear will be of value of when, in approaching a coast devoid of facilities for off-shore fixing, accuracy of the landfall is of particular importance.

Defence against Surface Forces and Submarines

17. Arrangements for defence against surface forces and submarines during the approach will be in general similar to those required during the voyage. Additional measures may, however, be required for protection against night attack by destroyers and motor torpedo boats. Cruiser and destroyer screens may be used for this purpose.

18. If the last part of the approach is effected in daylight, extensive anti-submarine operations, in addition to normal antisubmarine screening, may also be required.

Defence against Mines

19. Defence against mines will depend partly on protector paravanes, which will be streamed by transports and by all warships bigger than destroyers, and partly on the operations of minesweeping vessels, either destroyers or minesweepers. In view of the vulnerability of merchant ships to mine explosions and the possible failure of paravane protection, particularly during alterations of course, minesweeping operations will play a part in an approach through mineable waters. The ideal is to sweep a clear passage for the expedition, but if this is not practicable searching sweeps must be carried out sufficiently far ahead of the force to allow a detour to be made round any waters found to be mined.

20. As paravanes must be hoisted in before stopping, minesweeping will be of particular importance in the vicinity of the position from which the landing craft will leave the ships.

21. The efficiency of minesweeping at night does not fall far short of that achieved by day. To attain this efficiency, however it is necessary to show a few small lights, and there remains the slight danger of ships hitting mines whose

moorings have been cut sweepers. If the presence of a minefield is suspected in an area in which it is intended to operate at night, the mine risk must be balanced against the possible loss of surprise due to the use of lights. In circumstances of exceptional danger from minefields it may be necessary to postpone operations till daylight, despite the almost certain loss of surprise.

Defence against Aircraft

22. Arrangements for defence against aircraft during the approach will be in general similar to those for the voyage, direct protection being afforded by the A.A. gunfire of the escorting warships. When air opposition is probable the escort will include special anti-aircraft ships.

23. When the last part of the approach is effected in daylight, fighter patrols may be of value as an additional deterrent to air attack.

24. Should it be probable that, despite the steps taken to counter the enemy's reconnaissance, the expedition has been sighted on the afternoon previous to the landing and is being shadowed, the possibility of night attacks by aircraft must be considered. Every effort must be made by the use of fighter aircraft to destroy or drive off shadowing aircraft before dusk. On calm starlight nights aircraft can attack surface craft without requiring artificial aids to illuminate their targets, and during their attacks they remain mainly invisible to the crews of anti-aircraft weapons. Under better conditions of light (*i.e.* moonlight) it may be possible to engage them with close range A.A. weapons but at present it is unlikely that it will be possible to bring long-range A.A. weapons into play effectively. Little evidence is available as to the accuracy of bombing over the sea at night but it can be assumed that it is likely to be less accurate, height for height, than by day. The effectiveness of torpedo attack by aircraft on a convoy at night may be considerably reduced by stationing a screen of warships in such a way as to hamper the aircraft at the moment of dropping torpedoes.

Postponement

25. A change in the weather conditions or some other circumstances may require the operation to be postponed even in its final stages. Consideration must therefore be given to the means of communicating such a decision and of the action to be taken by all forces on its receipt.

[. . .]

Anti-aircraft Defence of the Landing by Ships' Gunfire

101. Direct protection against air attack on the ships carrying the assaulting force, whether warships or transports, will be afforded in the same way as during the voyage and approach, *i.e.,* by long-range and close-range A.A. weapons mounted in warships supplemented by close-range weapons mounted in transports.

102. The relative positions taken up by ships during transfer of troops to landing craft will need consideration from the point of view of affording the best protection with the weapons available.

103. In addition to attacking the ships, it is probable that enemy aircraft endeavouring to hamper the landing will carry out low-flying attacks on the landing craft and the troops disembarking from them. Arrangements must therefore be made for the warships providing covering fire to be so disposed as to provide anti-aircraft fire in the vicinity of the landing places, such arrangements being necessarily dependent on the ships being able to stand close enough in.

104. Under some conditions it may be advisable to employ destroyers specially equipped for A.A. work in addition to any destroyers or other vessels providing support by bombardment.

105. In addition to the protection provided by ships, close-range A.A. weapons may be mounted in some of the landing craft and in small craft accompanying them (M.T.Bs. or fast motor boats).

106. When motor lighters are employed in landing the assaulting troops, partial protection against low-flying machine gun attack may be provided by bullet-proof plating.

107. It is important that all ships, small craft and landing craft mounting A.A. weapons should be informed of the number and type of our own aircraft which are likely to be operating in the vicinity and the action to be expected from them in the presence of enemy aircraft.

Operations of Fighter Aircraft in Defence of the Landing

108. As has already been indicated, air superiority achieved by the main effort of our air forces can never guarantee that the enemy will not be able to operate any aircraft against either the ships of the expedition or the landing craft and assaulting troops. It may not be possible effectively to engage such aircraft with A.A. gunfire and consequently the employment of fighter aircraft in direct defence of the landing will have to be considered. Though fighter aircraft will not necessarily prevent attacks on the expedition, they will be able to hamper them considerably and in addition will be of value in enabling spotter and reconnaissance aircraft to do their work without molestation. The effectiveness of fighter patrols will be increased if arrangements, even though only partial, can be made to give them warning of the approach of enemy aircraft.

109. The aircraft required for these fighter patrols may be found by the Royal Air Force or the Fleet Air Arm or both. The operations of all fighters employed on this type of duty will be planned and controlled by the officer responsible for the co-ordination of air operations.

Aircraft for Strategical, Tactical and Artillery Reconnaissance for the Army

110. Instructions for operating aircraft in strategical, tactical and artillery reconnaissance for the army are contained in the Royal Air Force Manual of Army Co-operation and the War Office publication "The Employment of Air Forces with the Army in the Field." These instructions will be adhered to as far as possible, but may have to be modified in the following respects to adapt them to the conditions under which the operation is being conducted.

> (i) *Strategical reconnaissance.*—Where the expedition includes an Air Commander he will assume the responsibilities for strategical reconnaissance carried out by bombers normally undertaken by the commander of an air component of afield force.

> (ii) *Tactical and Artillery reconnaissance.*—It will not always be possible to employ Army Co-operation units in the normal manner in the early stages of the operations, but whatever expedients are adopted to overcome difficulties, the officers observing must always be fully trained Army Co-operation pilots, and the normal air liaison organization must be provided.

111. Whenever possible Army Co-operation units will be employed for tactical and artillery reconnaissance. Until landing operations have progressed sufficiently to cover advanced landing grounds ashore it is probable that the units will have to work from landing grounds separated by sea from the troops they are serving. Communications with these landing grounds will be an important matter for consideration. In some cases, however, it may be possible to improvise arrangements for overcoming the difficulties of operating Army Co-operation units from a distant landing ground by adopting one or other of the following expedients in the early stages:—

> (i) It may be possible to make arrangements for a certain number of sorties to fly off carriers. The disadvantage of this arrangement is that, at the conclusion of the reconnaissance, pilots would have to go back to their distant landing ground.

> (ii) Provided a carrier can be made available, Army Co-operation pilots may be trained in deck landing and operate from a carrier using Fleet Air Arm types of aircraft.

> (iii) Army Co-operation pilots may fly as observers in Fleet Air Arm aircraft operated from carriers by Fleet Air Arm pilots.

> (iv) It may be possible to do the reconnaissances required in the early stages with float-seaplanes, and to operate them from a seaplane tender in the vicinity of the landing.

One or more of these expedients may also on occasion have to be adopted to supplement normal Army Co-operation reconnaissances.

Naval Reconnaissance, Spotting and Anti-submarine Operations

112. Spotting for bombarding ships, naval reconnaissance and anti-submarine operations will be undertaken by Fleet Air Arm units, and in circumstances where the Royal Air Force undertake the gaining of air superiority will normally form the Fleet Air Arm's principal roles. The Fleet Air Arm units employed will be controlled by the Naval Commander. Though their operations will not usually need to be closely co-ordinated with those of other air units in the vicinity, they must be considered in relation to the general air plan; particularly to ensure that provision for the channels of communication they will require is made in the signal plan for the operations.

The Use of Aircraft for Supplies Dropping

113. When other means of getting ammunition and supplies to troops are not available, aircraft may be used to drop them by parachute. The use of aircraft for this purpose, however, may entail their absence from other and more important rôles, and this aspect must be given due consideration. Details of the method are to be found in the Royal Air Force manuals of Army Co-operation (A.P. 1176) and Supplies Dropping (A.P. 1180).

Co-ordination of Air Action during the Landing

114. Aircraft employed in neutralizing the enemy air forces will work either from established air stations, advanced air stations or carriers depending on the strategical situation.

115. The remaining air operations will need control by officers in direct touch with the landing. This can be exercised most efficiently if the aircraft work from ships or landing grounds close at hand. Unless there are aerodromes near enough for the purpose, it may be convenient to do as much as possible with aircraft from ships—either aircraft carriers, warships carrying seaplanes, or special seaplane carrying ships—until suitable sites or landing grounds have been captured during the progress of the landing operations.

116. In most cases aircraft taking part in the operations will be drawn both from the Royal Air Force and the Fleet Air Arm and their operations will need to be co-ordinated by the senior officer concerned. This may be the Air Commander in charge of all air operations connected with the expedition, including the covering operations to attain air superiority. Under some conditions, however, cover may be provided by operations of the air force not directly connected with the expedition and the local air operations may not be sufficiently extensive to need an Air Commander. In these cases co-ordination would be effected by the senior of the officers in charge of the various units or formations of aircraft under the control of the Naval and Military Commanders. The officer co-ordinating air action will normally exercise operational control of all aircraft taking part except those employed

on A.C. duties, spotting for bombarding ships, naval reconnaissance and anti-submarine duties.

117. When some or all of the aircraft under the orders of the Air Commander (or other officer co-ordinating air operations) are working from aircraft carriers, the operations of these aircraft are necessarily dependent to some extent on naval considerations. Under these conditions the Air Commander (or other officer co-ordinating air operations) will indicate the tasks that he wishes the aircraft to perform and the Naval Commander will instruct the senior officer of the aircraft carriers to operate in the manner best calculated for the performance of these tasks, having due regard to both the air and naval situations.

CHAPTER 3
AIRBORNE ASSAULT

The airborne operations of D-Day made a distinctive contribution to the overall success of Operation *Overlord*. Both the United States and Britain had garnered some operational experience of airborne missions in North Africa and Italy, especially in Operation *Husky* over Sicily in July 1943, which saw combat drops by both the US 82nd Airborne Division and the British 1st Airborne Division. Yet the scale of the D-Day airborne operations was beyond anything else previously tested. Three full airborne divisions would participate: the US 82nd and 101st Airborne and the British 6th Airborne, totalling some 20,000 troops. The men not only deployed in their thousands by parachutes, but also flew in via gliders, these being able to carry heavier equipment such as jeeps and pack artillery.

The experience of the airborne troops, who touched down in occupied territory hours before the main landing forces, tested the mettle of every man involved. The BBC correspondent Robert Barr famously captured the mood as British paras climbed aboard their aircraft:

> Their faces were darkened with cocoa; sheathed knives were strapped to their ankles; tommy guns strapped to their waists; bandoliers and hand grenades, coils of rope, pick handles, spades, rubber dinghies hung around them, and a few personal oddments, like the lad who was taking a newspaper to read on the plane. . . There was an easy familiar touch about the way they were getting ready, as though they had done it often before. Well, yes, they had kitted up and climbed aboard often just like this – twenty, thirty, forty times some of them, but it had never been quite like this before. This was the first combat jump for every one of them.

Many of the paratroopers would not live to see out the war, or at least survive it unscathed. The US paratroopers took about 2,500 casualties on D-Day itself, while the British 6th Airborne Division returned home the following September having suffered around 4,500 dead, wounded and missing.

The first extract below is from a US field manual, *Tactics and Techniques of Airborne Troops (FM 31-30),* one of the most comprehensive tactical airborne guides published during the war.

Tactics and Techniques of Airborne Troops (1942)

CHAPTER 2
PLANNING AND PREPARATION

9. GENERAL.—

    a. The task force commander conducts any preliminary operations necessary to create conditions favorable to execution of the mission assigned to the task force. He requests higher authority to conduct preliminary operations that are beyond means available to the task force. Preliminary operations include preparatory combat operations; establishment of bases; arrangements for movements and concentrations of troops, equipment, and supplies to departure points; detailed reconnaissance of the objective; and preparation of tactical plans. All preparations should be completed well in advance of the date of the operation. Within limits imposed by the necessity for secrecy, subordinate commanders should be given timely information of details of the plan in order that units may have sufficient time to adjust equipment and personnel requirements, prepare plans, and complete special training.

    b. The time required by air landing units for preparation and planning depends upon the extent of any reorganization and special training required for the projected operation, and the complexity of arrangements necessary to insure coordinated action with supporting troops, particularly with the air task force.

    c. Units of air landing troops, specially organized and trained in air landing operations, are better adapted to employment on air landing missions than are standard units. However, even air landing units require adjustments in organization and equipment for any specific mission.

    d. All troops require special training with air task forces and parachute troops prior to employment in air landing operations. Troops landing on a field out of contact with enemy ground forces require no special training other than loading, and unloading personnel and equipment into and rom planes.

    e. The principles discussed herein are applicable to standard units as well as to air landing units.

10. ORDERS AND INFORMATION FROM HIGHER HEADQUARTERS.—Commanders of air landing units are provided with orders and information from the task force commander giving them full knowledge of the following:

a. Hostile situation.

b. General plan of operations.

c. Forces involved.

d. Missions of the parachute troops, the air landing force, the air task force, and any ground or naval forces which may be involved in the operation.

e. Objective of each force.

f. Time of attack and scheme of maneuver of ground forces.

g. Combat aviation support missions.

h. Signal commimication arrangements between forces.

i. Means of identifying friendly agents in enemy territory and assistance to be furnished by them.

j. Other information necessary to insure coordinated action by all elements of the combined force.

11. INFORMATION OF ENEMY.—Plans of air landing units must be based on accurate and detailed information. Higher headquarters and the task force commander will provide intelligence summaries giving detailed Information of enemy activities in the combat area; the location, strength, armament, and character of the hostile force, and its capabilities to interfere with the operation; location of antiaircraft batteries and other defensive installations; composition and type of organized defenses of airdromes, landing fields, and other military and civil installations; characteristics and morale of the civilian population and its effectiveness as part of the defense force; location and types of obstacles used to obstruct possible landing areas; and the location of highly mobile hostile forces.

12. MAPS AND AERIAL PHOTOGRAPHS.—A comprehensive knowledge of the terrain is essential to formulation of detailed tactical plans. Careful study and analysis of aerial photographs of the area will disclose much of the detail of the hostile defensive positions. Every effort is made to distinguish between actual and dummy positions by the study of a series of photographs taken over period of time. Maps and aerial photographs of suitable scale are provided. Approximately 50 sets will be required to provide for distribution within an infantry battalion, to include rifle platoons and supporting weapons sections. One hundred sets will be required if distribution is to include squads. Unit commanders study these thoroughly to become familiar with landing

and alternate landing sites, towns, roads, streams, prepared defenses, and other terrain features of the combat area. Operation maps and sketches indicating routes, objectives, and other details of initial combat operations are furnished to. or prepared by, subordinate units down to include the platoon or smaller unit having a separate mission.

13. INITIAL OBJECTIVES.—Initial objectives of air landing units will usually include —

a. *Hostile prepared positions.*—Defensive positions in the immediate vicinity of the landing area that are capable of covering the area with small-arms fire will normally be assigned as objectives to the parachute troops. Positions beyond the immediate vicinity of the field will usually be assigned to units of the air landing force. The strength of the attacking unit will be based upon an estimate of the probable strength of the defending force. (This estimate in turn is based upon the size or extent of the defensive position.) Where defensive areas are isolated or separated, as will usually be the case, plans should provide for attack from the flank or rear.

b. *Antiaircraft guns.*—Although the supporting aviation attempts to destroy or neutralize all antiaircraft guns disclosed by aerial photographs or by preliminary operations, each gun position should be assigned as an objective of either the parachute troops or air landing troops arriving in the early echelons. Guns which have been temporarily silenced but not destroyed may return to action with serious effect against transport planes. If these guns can be captured in a serviceable condition, they can be put to good use against hostile aviation which will make every effort to attack fields being used by air landing troops.

c. *Hostile observation.*—With capture of hostile positions covering the landing field by small-arms fire, one of the enemy's principal means of defense against an air-borne attack will be long-range fires directed against the landing area. Therefore, initial objectives assigned to air landing troops will include all terrain affording observation over the landing area.

d. *Hostile reserves.*—Since air-borne troops are particularly vulnerable while landing and immediately thereafter, defending forces will make every effort to launch prompt counterattacks by local reserves. Air landing troops must be on the alert for these attacks. Initial plans for attack by air landing troops should provide for the presence of combat aviation over the landing area with the mission of striking immediately any enemy movement, especially that of hostile mechanized forces. In some situations it may be advisable to assign as initial objectives for air landing units terrain which commands known assembly positions of hostile reserves, in order to immobilize those reserves by fire pending the arrival of sufficient troops to attack and destroy them.

e. *Hostile communications.*—Objectives of supporting aviation and of parachute troops will include the radio communications of the landing field. Air landing troops are instructed to cut immediately all wire lines they locate, including buried cables which may have been located from aerial photographs. Interruption of hostile messenger routes and control of roads over which reserves may be moved are primary objectives of air landing troops.

f. *Hostile transportation.*—Lack of organic motor transportation is a great handicap to air-borne troops. Whenever possible, nearby motor parks will be included in the initial objectives for air landing units. Plans should provide for drivers for captured enemy vehicles, for motor mechanics, and for a supply of gasoline and easily removable parts, such as distributor heads and spark plugs, in order to put vehicles into service quickly.

14. *Meteorological Conditions.*—Climate and weather conditions of the combat area affect decisions regarding types of clothing, equipment, and rations, as well as flying and landing operations. Decisions regarding altitude of flight may also affect the type of individual clothing prescribed.

15. ORGANIZATION, EQUIPMENT, AND PERSONNEL.— Modifications in the organization and equipment of air landing units will usually be required for each specific mission. Based on these modifications, the task force commander will issue instructions relative to personnel and equipment to be left behind. Noncombatant personnel, such as clerks and cooks, do not accompany leading echelons. Unit equipment, such as large trucks, kitchen equipment, or other bulky items which cannot be transported or which can be dispensed with during initial phases of the operation, are eliminated. Motor-vehicle operating and maintenance personnel usually accompany leading echelons when there is likelihood of capture of enemy vehicles.

16. SUPPLY.—Because of the limited amount of equipment and supplies that can accompany air landing troops, provision for early and continuous replenishment of ammunition, food, water, medical, and other essential provisions is arranged by the task force commander. Needs of air landing troops are carefully calculated, and arrangements for supplying them are made between supply services, the transport element of the air task force, and air landing troops.

17. SECRECY.—The task force commander prescribes measures to insure that plans and preparations are kept secret. These measures include restricting

discussion of plans; prohibiting wearing of distinctive insignia, clothing, and equipment by airborne troops in the concentration area; removing unit insignia and markings from vehicles; and concealing concentration of troops, equipment, and supplies. Location of landing fields and the day and hour of enplaning are not announced during early phases of preparation. "D"-day and "H"-hour are announced on short notice just prior to the time set for the operation. Instruction which might disclose location of the combat area is deferred as long as practicable.

18. TREATMENT OF CIVILIANS IN OCCUPIED TERRITORY.

a. The task force commander prescribes measures relative to safeguarding enemy public and private property, and control and treatment of civilians in occupied territory.

b. Fraternization with civilians, unlawful seizure of property, and abuse of individuals, are forbidden. All men are instructed in proper behavior, and distinction is made between measures of military necessity and deliberate misconduct.

c. Operations of troops landing in an area in which the population is generally unfamiliar with the English language may be facilitated by providing each soldier with a "phrase sheet" listing useful phrases and their phonetic equivalent in the foreign language, e.g., "Give me water." The phonetic Spanish equivalent is "Dajonay agwa." The following are examples of phrases which may be useful:

"Give me water; food; map; match: gasoline."

"What is the name of this town? River?"

"Which way to the airport? Railroad? Station? Docks?"

"Guide me to ..."

"Keep off the road."

"Come here."

"Stay in your home."

"Halt."

"Walk in front of me."

"Stay where you are."

"Move along."

"Surrender your weapons; ammunition."

"Hold up your hands."

Personnel speaking the language of the country in which the operations are conducted should be attached to all air landing units.

19. EVACUATION.—Plans do not usually provide for evacuation of wounded from the combat area during the early stages of an air landing operation. Leading echelons of air landing troops include attached medical personnel and limited amounts of medical equipment and essential supplies. Tactical plans provide for the establishment of unit aid stations immediately after landing, usually in the vicinity of the landing area. Evacuation of wounded by plane or other transportation is initiated by the task force commander as soon as the situation permits.

20. COMMUNICATION.—

a. *General.*—The task force commander coordinates communication within the task force by means of signal operation instructions. Special measures are prescribed to insure rapid and positive communication between elements of supporting aviation, parachute troops and air landing troops. Generally, duplicate means of communication between air elements and ground forces are prescribed to insure continuity of communication.

b. *Communication between air landing troops and supporting aviation.*— Parachute troops and air landing troops maintain communication with supporting aviation in order to keep the air elements advised of the ground situation, and to be able to call for support, ammunition, food, and other essential supplies where and when needed. Communication between ground and air forces is effected by means of radio, panels, pyrotechnics, and such other means as may be available or improvised. For communication between aircraft and landed troops in close contact with the enemy, codes and signals for prearranged phrases improvised for a particular operation are frequently used. These must be simple, practical, and limited in number, otherwise they will have little combat utility. Whatever the system of communication employed, it is essential that all ground troops, pilots, and air observers receive combined training in its use prior to the operation. All personnel of the task force should keep in mind the possibility of communication codes falling into the hands of the enemy and being used by him to his own advantage, perhaps to direct fire against our own troops. All concerned, particularly combat aviation, must be alert to detect such action. An intimate knowledge of the plans and methods of operation of ground troops by pilots of combat planes minimizes the likelihood of their responding to false calls. Improvised signals and codes outlined hereafter are not prescribed but are included merely as illustrative examples.

(1) *Panel communication with combat aircraft.*—Only advance elements of attacking ground forces display marking panels when held up by enemy resistance or when requested to do so by friendly aircraft. Combat aviation, familiar with the general direction of advance of attacking forces, searches the terrain in front of the indicated front-line troops, and without special request attacks any hostile positions discovered. Ground troops may direct the attention of supporting combat planes to targets by displaying panels in pre-arranged code. Likewise, other prearranged messages may be transmitted by panel code. (See fig. 1.) The code shown is illustrative only.

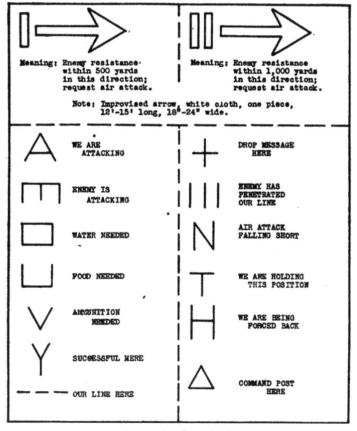

Figure 1. Sample panel code

(2) *Use of pyrotechnics.*—

    (a) *Plane to ground.*—By means of a prearranged color code, aircraft using the Very pistol may signal ground troops to "mark front line," "mark battalion headquarters," and other definite items.

    (b) *Ground to plane.*—Ground troops may signal aircraft by the use of colored ground flares, ground signal projectors, and smoke. For example, the direction to targets might be indicated by establishing the line with two or more smoke pots or flares appropriately separated, or by means of an arrow improvised from panels or other white material.

(3) *Air-ground voice radio.*—

    (a) In operations involving close support by combat aviation, time is a vital factor, therefore messages may be sent in the clear. Adoption of a coded templet or map-coordinates code for giving coordinates offers a high degree of secrecy with a minimum loss of time. All participating units (ground and air) must use identical equipment for this purpose. A prearranged form for requests increases the degree of secrecy, serves to brief the message, and expedites its transmission. A model for this form follows:

        1. Designation of target, including location by a coded templet or map-coordinate code.

        2. Time of attack (time bracket) .

        3. Bomb safety line, if necessary.

        4. Special instructions.

        5. Time signed and signature.

The *Parachute Training Manual* was produced by the British Air Ministry in March 1944, just a few months before the D-Day operations. It is a comprehensive work, its topics ranging from the practicalities of specific parachute types to the challenges for pilots of dropping 'sticks' of men in the right place at the right time. The foreword to the manual acknowledges that training paratroopers involves far more than just teaching them jump skills. It stated that:

> *The training of soldiers as paratroopers involves two distinct requirements:–*
>
> (i) *Specialised Army weapon, ground and tactical training of which some of the more important aspects are demolition work, signals procedure, emplaning and deplaning of supplies, night operations, employment of captured enemy weapons and transport, use of foreign languages and so on.*
>
> (ii) *Training in parachute jumping, of which the various phases are discussed in this manual.*

It was this spectrum of training, based on the requirements of tactical self-sufficiency (paratroopers would typically spend many hours fighting alone before connecting with overland forces), plus the arduous nature of the physical training, that gave the airborne soldiers their elite status. As the extract below reveals, much was also expected of the pilots whose job it was to deliver the men to the right place at the right time.

Parachute Training Manual (1944)

TECHNIQUE OF DROPPING
General Principles

24. Although a pilot at a Parachute Training School carries out much repetition flying, this does not mean that the flying lacks interest. On the contrary, the technique of dropping paratroops is a subject of considerable interest because so many factors not met with in normal flying and bombing are involved. Knowledge and judgment will in time enable a pilot to drop his troops at a known landing ground with an accuracy which a new pilot cannot attain. And this skill can only be acquired by experience and application. It can be compared with the art of the old boatman who knows the currents on a particular stretch of water so well that he can, without effort, steer his boat to the spot he desires. The dropping of paratroops can properly be termed an art because the pilot who shows a special interest, or possesses a special aptitude, excels over the pilot who does not.

25. The aim when dropping paratroops is for the paratroop to jump so that he lands on a predetermined spot. An actual spot is not practicable, but a circle with a radius of 50 yards should be aimed at, and with skill, may be achieved. Success can be attained only if both the pilot and the paratroop act correctly; therefore, co-operation and mutual understanding between the pilot and paratroop is essential. Given this basis, the difficulties of accurate

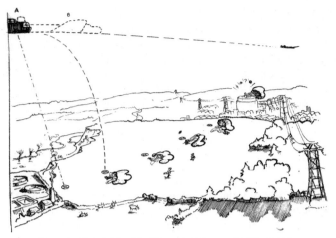

Figure 33. Signal delay (The National Archives, ref AIR10/3845)

dropping are still great, as compared with bombing, for a variety of reasons which are discussed under five headings below.

The Problem of Accurate Flying

26. This problem can be explained most easily by a simple example. Assume a pilot wishes to drop a paratroop on a particular spot when flying straight into a 15 m.p.h. wind at 500 ft. The amount of drift of a parachute descending at 18 ft. per second is shown by the table (Table I in para. 30) as 183 yards. The pilot therefore should approach the chosen landing spot in a straight line dead into wind. When he has left the spot 183 yards behind (ignoring for the moment all other factors) he should release his paratroop. The difficulties in this case are for the pilot–

   (i) to know when he is exactly over the landing spot;

   (ii) to fly a straight course into wind for 183 yards thereafter (in practice for the reasons stated in paras. 27 and 28 later he will not have to fly as far as 183 yards);

   (iii) to maintain accuracy of height whilst flying this course.

   (iv) to maintain a constant air speed.

With most aircraft, there will be a tendency, as a stick of paratroops leaves, for the aircraft to become nose heavy and for the air speed to increase. This tendency must be guarded against by the pilot. [. . .] The results can be disastrous for the last men and serious for the operational efficiency of the others.

The Problem of Signal Delay

27. The normal method by which a pilot gives the signal to jump is by pressing an electric switch which shows a green light in the cabin of the aircraft, on seeing which the Despatcher gives the order to the first paratroop to jump. This sequence obviously involves a time lag from the moment the pilot has made up his mind that he has reached the spot required, to the moment the paratroop actually leaves the aircraft. Three human brains and physical reactions are involved, and a time lag of one or more seconds may occur. For this lag again the pilot must make allowance, though it is difficult to predict the correct amount unless the pilot knows his passengers and their time reactions.

The diagram at fig. 33 shows a drop in conditions of no wind. The aircraft pilot made up his mind that he was at the right spot when he was nearly over it at A but by the time he had pressed the switch and the first paratroop had left at "B," there was a delay of 3 seconds during which time the aircraft covered 150 yards (*see* Table II). To this has to be added the throw forward of the paratroop on leaving (perhaps 90 yards) and a slow stick, with the result that the last jumper finds himself landed outside the intended dropping area.

The Problem of Point of Departure

28. The drift table (Table I in para. 30) assumes that the paratroop jumps from a stationary object at a known height and that his parachute is fully open at that height. In actual fact, he jumps from a moving aircraft the height above the ground may not be precisely known, and the parachute is not fully developed for a period of 2–3 seconds after jumping. During this delay the paratroop has fallen about 100 ft., and he has been carried forward as a result of his jump and the speed (120 m.p.h.) of the aircraft from which he jumped, for about 90 yards. It will be seen, therefore, how many factors under this heading alone exist to upset the pilot's calculations.

The diagram (fig. 34) illustrates how an aircraft dropping in a slight following wind, has failed to make allowance for the throw forward and wind, with the result that the last paratroop is landed beyond the spot intended.

The Problem of Rate of Descent

29. This is one of the greatest difficulties because it will be affected by up and down currents of air, by the performance and shape of the parachute, by the weight of the parachute, and by other unpredictable factors. Up and down currents are caused both by turbulence and wind, and they will vary from day to day and from hour to hour. In time, the experienced pilot at a school will learn, after dropping his first stick, what the effect of such currents is likely to be at any particular time and day, and adapt his dropping technique accordingly. In certain atmospheric conditions, however, it will be difficult to make accurate allowance for such currents. Such conditions are particularly

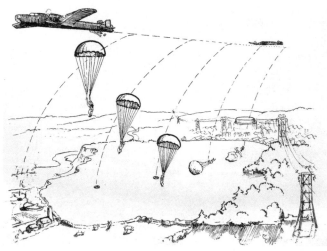

Figure 34. Point of departure (The National Archives, ref AIR10/3845)

prevalent in tropical countries where it may happen that the first jumper of a stick is supported sufficiently long by an up current for him to land after the last jumper in the stick.

Oscillation or delayed development of the parachute will also affect its rate of descent and these factors will be impossible to predict accurately. The effect of the weight of a paratroop on rate of descent is discussed in Chapter III, para. 49, but this is not of great account if the jump is made from a low height.

The diagram (fig. 35) shows various factors which can affect the rate and direction of descent of paratroops as follows :–

No. 1.	Oscillation.
No. 2.	Gusts
No. 3.	Delayed opening.
No. 4.	Normal descent.
No. 5.	Air currents off hillside.

The Problem of Drift

30. The drift table at Table I indicates the position at which a 28-ft. parachute will land if it floats down at varying known rates of descent from a stationary object (such as the top of a tower), and if both the rate of, descent and the drift are constant. Unfortunately none of these factors are constant, and therefore the drift table must be taken merely as a general guide to what is likely to happen, and not as a guide to what will in fact happen. The drift will

Figure 35. Rate of descent (The National Archives, ref AIR10/3845)

be affected by variations in the strength and directions of the wind between the aircraft and the ground. Whilst it is impossible in practice for a pilot to prejudge these variations at an unknown D.Z., he should in time gain considerable knowledge of them at his own school dropping ground. If available, a rear gunner can usually provide the most accurate estimation of drift.

The diagram at fig. 36 indicates how a pilot, dropping across wind has failed to allow enough for drift.

Stick Dropping

31. The principles governing the dropping of sticks do not vary in any way from those governing the dropping of individuals. The success of putting down a stick accurately will depend almost entirely on whether the first man is dropped correctly. In stick dropping, however, the effect of wind direction and strength assumes greater importance than with single drops, and the difficulties of accurate flying are increased by the effect on trim which the dropping of 10 or more men may involve. As the paratroops leave the aircraft, it will normally become nose heavy thus tending to increase the airspeed and cause a loss of height which must at all costs be avoided. Steep turns before the dropping run must also be avoided and particularly excess speed. One of the best ways to lose excess speed if it can be done without affecting the jumper or deployment of the parachute, is to lower the flaps or undercarriage, or both.

It is preferable to fly either into wind or across wind when dropping paratroops. With stick dropping, down-wind flying should always be avoided,

Figure 36. Drift (The National Archives, ref AIR10/3845)

otherwise the length of the stick on the ground will be greatly increased. A simple example will illustrate this point. Assume that a stick of 10 has to be dropped and that it will take 10 seconds for them to leave the aircraft which will fly at 110 m.p.h. with a wind of 15 m.p.h. The graph at fig. 37 shows that if flying into wind, the ground distance covered by the aircraft during the stick exit—which will be the length of the stick on the ground—is 465 yards, whilst if flying down wind the length is 611 yards.

From the point of view of the pilot, a beam wind is probably the easiest as he only has to calculate and allow for drift at 90° to his track.

Dropping sticks in wind directions which are not either into wind or across wind involves risks which should not be taken unless the dropping area is large, the wind strength is slight, or the pilot very experienced.

32. When dropping into wind it is a safe and simple rule to put on the red light to stop jumping when the end of the dropping area is reached. But when dropping down wind the last paratroop must leave at a distance before the end of the dropping area greater than the length of his drift. This is due to the invariable time lag in communication between the pilot and the paratroop and the initial forward fall of the paratroop. Thus in calm, beam, or down-wind conditions, it is advisable for the pilot to put on the stop light for jumping before the last safe spot is actually reached.

It is useful for pilots to set a stop watch or count at 1 second intervals during team exits so that they may know when the last man of their stick

TABLE I. Table of Variation in Drift for Different Dropping Heights, Wind Speeds and Rates of Descent

Height of Drop Rates of Descent in Feet per Second	Wind Speed 5 m.p.h.			Wind Speed 10 m.p.h.			Wind Speed 15 m.p.h.			Wind Speed 20 m.ph		
	16	18	20	16	18	20	16	18	20	16	18	20
300 ft...	38.3	34.0	30.6	76.6	68.0	61.2	114.8	102.1	91.9	153.1	136.0	122.5
400 ft...	53.6	47.6	42.9	107.2	95.3	85.7	160.7	142.9	128.6	214.4	190.4	171.5
500 ft...	68.9	61.2	55.1	137.8	122.5	110.2	206.6	183.7	165.4	275.6	244.8	220.5
600 ft...	84.2	74.9	67.4	168.5	149.7	134.7	252.5	224.5	202.1	336.9	299.2	269.5
700 ft...	99.5	88.5	79.6	199.1	176.9	159.2	298.4	265.3	238.9	398.1	353.6	318.5
800 ft...	114.8	102.1	91.9	229.7	204.1	183.7	344.3	306.1	275.6	459.4	408.0	367.5
900 ft...	130.1	115.7	104.1	260.3	231.4	208.2	390.2	346.9	312.4	520.6	462.4	416.5
1,000 ft.	145.4	129.3	116.4	291.0	258.6	232.7	436.1	387.8	349.1	581.9	516.8	465.5

D = 0.49 W/V (H−50)

W = Wind Speed—m.p.h.

D = Drift in yards.

H = Dropping Height—in feet.

V= Rate of Descent—per/sec.

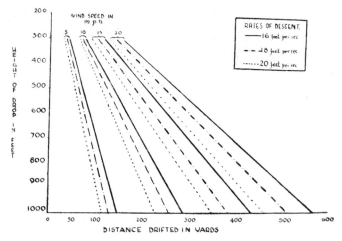

Figure 37 (The National Archives, ref AIR10/3845)

ought to have left the aircraft: alternatively, at a school, the Despatcher can indicate to the pilot by switching a light in the cockpit or by inter com.

Formation Dropping

33. This is a requirement of school training because it gives paratroops company training on the ground after landing. This is necessary since on daylight operations, it may well prove essential to put a large number of paratroops onto the ground in a very short space of time if they are to be capable of effective action. This can only be done by formation flying. The principles governing formation dropping are similar to those already set out but greater responsibility rests on the leading aircraft which will normally control the dropping.

There are two main types of formation that can be used—line astern and Vic—and their use is governed entirely by the requirements of the drop.

34. *Line astern formation* is particularly suitable in long, narrow dropping areas, and where the number of aircraft is not too great. It allows for great manoeuvrability on the part of the aircraft, but interference from slip stream may affect the following aircraft so that they will have to "step-up" or "step-down" according to the type of aircraft. If they have to "step up," the last aircraft may find itself so high that accurate dropping is difficult, or alternatively, "stepping-down" may not allow the rear aircraft sufficient dropping height. In practice, it is best to avoid "stepping-up" or "down" if the slip-stream difficulties can be overcome. In this kind of formation, each pilot has the opportunity to use his own judgment for releasing his paratroops.

TABLE II Distance covered per second by an aircraft at a given air-speed and wind-speed.

Air Speed (m.p.h.)	Wind Speed (m.p.h.)	Ground Speed (m.p.h.)	Distance covered per second yards.
Flying Up Wind			
90	15	75	36.6
90	10	80	39.1
90	5	85	41.5
100	15	85	41.5
100	10	90	44.0
100	5	95	46.5
110	15	95	46.5
110	10	100	49.0
110	5	105	51.3
120	15	105	51.3
120	10	110	54.0
120	5	115	56.2
Flying In Calm			
90	Nil	90	44.0
100	Nil	100	49.0
110	Nil	110	54.0
120	Nil	120	58.7
Flying Down Wind			
90	5	95	46.5
90	10	100	49.0
90	15	105	51.3
100	5	105	51.3
100	10	110	54.0
100	15	115	56.2
110	5	115	56.2
110	10	120	58.7
110	15	125	61.1
120	5	125	61.1
120	10	130	63.5
120	15	135	66.0

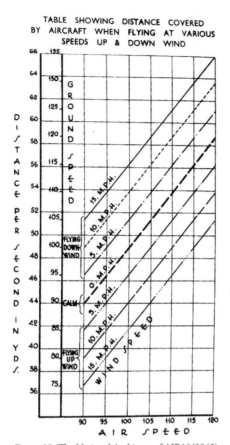

Figure 38 (The National Archives, ref AIR10/3845)

35. *Vic formation* in flights of three or five aircraft allows for greater concentration of aircraft over the dropping area in a given space of time, combined with more compact patterns on the ground. This formation is not so manoeuvrable as Line Astern and is difficult for reducing speed; therefore, correct adherence to the line of approach and a steady air speed on the approach are essential, and a correspondingly greater responsibility rests on the Leader. Close formations of five aircraft in Vic formation are in advisable, except for demonstration purpose sat a known dropping ground.

36. To obtain concentration of paratroops on the ground in an exercise or on operations, Squadron Vic formation of three aircraft is probably the best procedure. Providing the leader of the Vic drops accurately, the pilots

on his flanks may be comparatively inexperienced, for they can release their paratroops simultaneously with their leader, either by visual timing or under R/T instructions. So long as they are in good formation, the ultimate pattern on the ground will be compact.

Exercise Dropping

37. The final application of dropping technique arrives when a team and containers have to be landed after a cross-country flight at an unfamiliar dropping zone. To his dropping skill the pilot must add the expert use and appreciation of large scale maps (1 in. to 1 mile) and mosaic photographs. If possible the selected area must be photographed by a vertical air camera and the area compared and transferred to the large scale map. From this map the height above sea level of the area may be determined. Several considerations affect the "run-in," perhaps the foremost being the shape of the area; obstructions, wind speed and direction are also vital factors. The selected track of the stick is eventually plotted on the 1-in. map, and the line extended to form a "line of approach" of about 5 miles in length and preferably terminating at some easily recognisable pin-point. This pin-point is then co-ordinated to the smaller scale map, and its track and distance measured. Normal cross-country navigation is employed to reach this pin-point, after which the aircraft is headed on the run-in to the dropping area. Wind speed and direction will have been previously estimated, but must be carefully checked so that a course may be set to make good the track of the run-in. Height and air speed are reduced; close and accurate map-reading, together with timing, are then essential in order to bring the aircraft precisely over the correct and pre-determined point on the boundary of the field where dropping is to be carried out. It is not possible, especially in formation, to make last moment alterations of course, but, provided the line of approach is made absolutely accurate some way from the D.Z., the aircraft should arrive at the correct point of the dropping area at the proper height, airspeed and time, and drop the "stick" on the first run across. In any case, it is usually better to drop on an incorrect area the first time than circle trying to find the exact location.

Night Dropping

38. The technique of dropping by night is similar to that already described for day flying.

When dropping at D.Zs. other than a school dropping ground, low-flying cross-country navigation will be more difficult than by day and it will be essential to carry a navigator. He must assume full responsibility for the run up and dropping signals, as the pilot will be occupied with his flying, and in particular, in ensuring that he is not flying too fast at the moment of jumping. There will in any case be a tendency to fly too fast at night which will be accentuated by the need to lose height which will usually be necessary just before the drop.

There will be greater difficulty in judging the correct duration of the green light and the moment at which to switch on the "stop" signal, particularly on dark nights when obstructions are hardly discernible. If several aircraft are dropping over the same D.Z. they should fly at different heights.

Wind direction and strength are more difficult to assess by night than by day. But wind strength and air currents are likely to be less at night, which will assist accuracy in dropping.

Water Dropping

39. Dropping into water is very similar to dropping on to land. Movement of the surface of the water will afford a guide to wind speed and direction, but this will be difficult to assess unless the wind is fairly high.

For training purposes a boat can be stationed in the middle of the area and if it can ride at anchor, it will form a good wind indicator. It is inadvisable to use a smoke indicator, as in light airs the smoke will tend to lie on the surface, and so hinder the work of rescue craft.

The continuity of the dropping is dependant upon the speed at which the paratroops are picked up by the rescue launch, which in turn is governed by the accuracy with which the pilot drops. It is helpful to the pilot, if after reaching a parachute, the launch will retain its position relative to the marker boat, in order that the pilot may later gauge the drift for his next drop.

40. The depth of the water is important as paratroops must not be dropped into shallow water which may be present round the edges of a lake, nor into water which contains obstructions. In these circumstances markers may be necessary and additional care exercised by the pilot. Providing rescue facilities are adequate, there to need be no limit as the number dropped in a "stick."

Dropping into water at night without aids is not difficult if there is moonlight as this defines the water area clearly.

4. METHODS OF DROPPING

41. Various systems that can be employed for dropping paratroops are as follows:—

    (i) Judgment by air crew.

    (ii) Judgment by paratroop section leader

    (iii) Ground markings.

    (iv) Paratroop sight.

    (v) Radio.

Each method is briefly discussed below.

Judgement by Air Crew

42. At a school, if this method is adopted, the pilot will probably have to rely on his own judgment alone, assisted perhaps by ground markings, and he will be responsible for operating the signals which control the jumping. If a full air crew is carried the bomb-aimer navigator will be given the responsibility of controlling the run up and the dropping of signals.

43. The most useful aid to a pilot dropping by judgement is a smoke indicator in the form of a candle or generator let into the ground in the centre of the dropping area. Such an aid is closely related to natural conditions, and is valuable telling the pilot the strength and direction of the wind on the ground. It is the aid most generally useful as it may well be possible to use smoke at or near an operational dropping ground.

At known dropping ground, such as is used by a school, it is normally satisfactory to allow pilots to drop by judgement alone, unless strong or erratic winds are blowing. But if this method is adopted for exercises, experienced pilots should be used, and it is incumbent on them to make themselves fully acquainted with the D.Z. and the weather conditions at the spot before taking off. D.Zs vary greatly in difficulty and they should be selected for advanced training according to the standard of the pilot.

If the weather conditions on any particular day are expected to be difficult, it is helpful to drop a dummy before live jumps start.

The previous section has indicated difficulties connected with dropping by judgment alone. Fortunately these are not, in practice, as great as might be expected, unless dropping takes place from a considerable height, because some of the problems will cancel out each other.

44. The following are useful rules for air crews :—

    (a) Always start an accurate run-up at least one mile from the dropping ground. In the case of D.Zs the run up must be much longer.

    (b) During the run-up and dropping never skid or make any other sudden alteration in the course of the aircraft.

    (c) Continue straight flight some distance after the dropping ground.

    (d) If not formating, never follow too closely in the wake of an aircraft in front.

    (e) Jumping nearly always starts too late rather than too early.

    (f) A pilot should always, if circumstances permit, look at the result of his drops, and if the paratroops have not landed where he intended, find out the reason why.

(g) A pilot should always know the standard of the paratroops he is carrying.

45. Interest in the standard of dropping can be increased by a system of marks awarded to pilots for accuracy of dropping. This can conveniently be carried out at a school when the trainees are dropping in pairs. An area is marked on the ground within which the first of each pair should land, marks being awarded according to the distance from the centre of the circle that the landing is made.

A record should always be kept of inaccurate dropping so that unreliable pilots can be identified and if necessary removed.

Judgment by Paratroop Section Leader

46. This system is employed occasionally on aircraft using a door exit (*e.g.*, C.47). The leader of the paratroop section is known as the jump-master. During careful briefing of the pilot and jump-master—usually with the assistance of aerial photographs of the dropping zone— a pin-point is selected from which the pilot is to make his run-up to the dropping zone; the direction of the run-up is settled, and the jump-master, having due regard to wind conditions, selects some landmark opposite the door of the aircraft at which he will commence dropping his stick. When the pilot arrives at the selected pin-point he switches a signal light and the jump-master (No. 1) stands at the door; looking out. When he sees the selected landmark opposite to him, he jumps and the rest of the stick follows him. In this case the responsibility for the placing of the stick rests with the jump-master and not with the pilot or observer.

Ground Markings

47. The employment of ground markings useful at a busy school as it assists accurate dropping by all aircraft. A satisfactory system of ground signals is as follows:

A smoke indicator in the centre of the dropping ground is an added convenience to indicate the strength and direction of the wind at ground level.

48. The Officer in charge of the dropping area is responsible

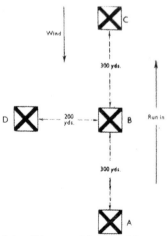

Figure 39. (The National Archives, ref AIR10/3845)

for laying out the ground signals and in doing this he is guided by exactly the same principles as those governing the pilot who is dropping by judgment. It is desirable for the chief pilot at least to be in wireless communication with the officer in charge of the dropping area so that the position of the ground markings can be altered if necessary. Good co-operation between them can result in great accuracy when dropping large numbers of troops.

Additional ground signals and means of communication between the aircraft and officer in charge of the dropping ground are explained in Chapter VI.

The use of ground markings is apt to make pilots slack in their appreciation of the problems of dropping, and this fact must be watched at a school where the use of such markings may be desirable owing to employment of inexperienced pilots or to large output. It is also necessary to have a clearly defined responsibility for laying out the ground signals and for changing them if they are found to be incorrectly placed.

Glider operations were another species of airborne action, the gliders offering very different capabilities than paratroopers. The advantages of gliders was not just the carrying capacity of the aircraft for vehicles, artillery pieces and other heavy equipment, but also the fact that that the dozen or so airborne troops inside could be landed at one destination with weapons at the ready and without the dispersal of a parachute 'stick'. The glider approach was also silent, reducing the risk of their detection on the approach. Total range of a glider following release from the tow aircraft varied considerably according to release altitude and weather conditions, but was in the region of 5–10 miles. The two main gliders used on D-Day were the US Waco CG-4, which could carry 13 troops, a jeep and crew, or a 75mm pack howitzer and crew, or the British Airspeed Horsa and General Aircraft Hamilcar. The British Horsa had similar properties to the CG-4, albeit with a heavier carrying capacity (up to 25 troops), but the Hamilcar was a massive glider capable of carrying a light tank. Although gliders had their advantages, they had plenty of issues to contend with, such as poor handling under loads, susceptibility to high winds, and a tendency to break apart on rough landings.

Glider Manual (1942)

Method of Attack

68. The order of operations for an airborne attack might be on the following lines:–

(a) Air Reconnaissance.

(b) Bombing of enemy fighter aerodromes, and of R.D.F. stations as a vital part of fighter defence, perhaps over several days.

(c) Intensified bombing as above, on the night preceding the attack.

(d) Vigorous dive-bombing at dawn on ground defences, in successive waves, to disclose the small-arms defences of the area.

(e) Ground-strafing by waves of fighters on the defences disclosed;

(f) Landing of parachute troops shortly after the above, possibly accompanied by gliders, with fighter screen, and with standing patrols of dive-bombers and fighters ready to support ground troops when signalled for assistance. These landings might begin before the bombing attack ended, whilst it was lifted in the immediate landing areas only.

(g) Glider-borne troops arrive shortly after parachute troops, who have prepared the ground. Fighter cover continues.

(h) Troop-carrying aeroplanes might land on prepared ground.

A US Army Air Force Waco CG-4A-WO glider.

(i) Large scale sabotage and diversion operations might be carried out simultaneously.

(j) Land support (or evacuation) follows.

Light and Weather

69. The need for good weather is a serious limitation to glider-borne operations. The weather must be such as to give good serviceability of aerodromes, favourable wind direction for the journey, moderate wind strength if parachutes are to be used, and good visibility at least for landing. If a large formation is to be launched to arrive simultaneously, visibility must be good, but small successive waves might make use of bad visibility and cloud cover in which a large formation would involve undue risk of collision. Vulnerability in the air would be much reduced. But bad visibility near the ground (mist or fog) would make landing extremely difficult, and the full use of cloud cover depends on the successful development of blind towing.

70. The great advantages of launching an attack by daylight are obvious, e.g., preliminary assembly, emplaning, take-off, assembly at rendezvous and accurate navigation are simplified. But an airborne attack carried out wholly in daylight against a well defended area could be very costly.

70A. If the landing is to be at dusk or shortly after nightfall, weather forecasts can be relied on to a much greater extent than for a dawn landing. Reconnaissance aircraft may have been able to obtain up-to-date information for an evening landing, but the weather may change considerably overnight before a dawn landing. The evening landing also allows enemy fighters to be grounded during the attack as a result of intensive fighter and bomber sweeps during the day.

71. Landing at dusk has all the advantages and disadvantages of full daylight take-off and approach. To land in exactly the right light, in reasonable visibility without too great a delay before advantage can be taken of darkness, requires very careful timing. The smaller the force, the simpler this task. The airborne force, knowing its tasks exactly and having some hours of darkness to assemble and concentrate, has a distinct advantage over the enemy. The latter cannot be certain of the objective, and must collect and handle reserves in the dark. Above all, the attackers are largely immune from air attack. The disadvantage to the attackers of having to move in the dark is by no means a serious one to well-trained troops who have studied the ground intimately from maps, air photographs and models. The half hour or more of twilight which is available after landing affords a good opportunity to get the lie of the land and to start concentrating.

72. To land early in the night just after it gets dark gives the advantages of a daylight take-off, and the attackers still have some hours of darkness at their disposal. [But glider-borne attack by night have not yet been proved feasible, and in addition to being risky as regards the actual landing, depends on the successful development of night towing. The take-off might be organised in good moonlight conditions, assembly in the air being assisted by signal lights or wireless from the air or from the ground. But a landing even in moonlight might result in high casualties. Flares could hardly be used for landing in a surprise operation. A dawn landing is more likely. A preceding force of parachutists might however be put down at night, night dropping is highly developed.]

73. The advantages in approaching and landing at night are as follow:

    (a) No fighter escorts are required.

    (b) Aimed Flak can be largely avoided.

    (c) The enemy is unable to locate the landing areas immediately.

The main disadvantages of a night take-off and landing are:-

    (a) The added complication of night assembly take-off.

    (b) A greatly decreased rate of take-off and landing and the impossibility of flying in formation so that the force arrives in driblets.

    (c) The difficulty of accurate navigation by night. Even prominent landmarks, such as water, white cliffs and isolated woods can only be seen in clear conditions and bright moonlight. Searchlights, gun flashes and bright fires greatly increase the difficulty of seeing ground at night.

74. Landings at dawn entail the same disadvantages given (a) to (b) above. Very accurate timing is essential; the enemy are very much in the alert from first light if airborne attack is at all likely; as the light grows, the landings are liable to air attack which may seriously interfere with assembly and concentration. Accurate navigation may still be difficult at dawn owing to ground mist; flak although not so accurate as in full daylight will be more effective than at night. However, the attackers can see what they are doing: confusion is less likely and the objectives should be more speedily reached.

Assembly and Take-off

75. Success or failure in most operations of war depends very much on correct timing, and exact adherence to that timing. Especially is this so with Airborne Forces, which co-operate intimately with the R.A.F. and in fact, depend on it for transport. The hour at which a unit or sub-unit is timed to pass a point, reach an assembly area or aerodrome, and emplane, is worked out to ensure exact co-ordination of the operation as a whole. A Commander who fails to function up to time may jeopardise not only the lives of those under his command but the success of the whole operation.

76. It has been held that the collection of gliders on aerodromes for a major operation would be so conspicuous as to offer an easy target for bombing, especially as it might be necessary to stand by for favourable weather, But this need not be so if the gliders are dispersed over several aerodromes, as they must be if a large force is to take off within a reasonable time. The force might assemble in peace at far rearward aerodromes, and on the day previous to the operation, given a good weather forecast, be towed to a forward base where aircraft would be marshalled (perhaps at night) for take-off at dawn. This procedure was followed by the enemy in the invasion of Crete.

77. The length of time between the first landing at the objective and complete assembly as an organised force is of first importance. The speed with which the whole force can be put into the air therefore is a vital factor, since the total landing time will depend on the total take-off time. A further reason for shortening the take-off time is that troops going into action should not be kept seated in aircraft too long. The total landing time can be roughly estimated by picturing the formation in the air, and dividing its length by its ground speed. Appreciation of the importance of short total take-off time no doubt accounts for the very long runways which the Germans have built at many aerodromes, which allow for the marshalling of large numbers of gliders in addition to the actual take-off run. The runway at Stavanger is already over 2,000 yards long and has been doubled in width. Runway aerodromes seem essential for any large scale operation.

78. On such a runway, given well-trained ground crews, twenty 25-seater gliders, arranged in order of priority of take-off as on an aircraft carrier, might

assemble in 600 yards, with their tugs, leaving over 1200 yards for the actual take-off run. With reasonably good organisation and freedom from mishaps, all the aircraft might take off within twenty minutes. Thirty such aerodromes could deal with a fleet of 600 to 800 gliders carrying an airborne force of 10,000 men and their equipment. For reasons of navigation and protection, such a fleet would probably proceed in mass formations. Prompt assembly in the air is therefore important. If the take-off were before first light, aircraft with tail lights might follow one another to the air rendezvous where the whole fleet would converge. Alternatively, the fleet might proceed in a series of waves. Beacon lights might be set within friendly territory to absorb initial errors of timing. Radio homing devices might be used, being either dropped by parachute from an aeroplane on to the objective or nearby, giving automatic signals, or being operated by agents in or near the landing area or at the release point.

Methods of Towing and Approach

79. Three methods of towing and approach seem to be offered:-

(a) Towing to the required height to allow release long distance from the landing area.

This method has the advantages of likelier surprise and earlier release of the tug for further duty; the tug does not come within range of ground or air defences near the objective; the period of tow, during which both aircraft are more vulnerable, is shortened.

From the point of release, the gliders should be within sight of one another. Experienced navigators would lead the way, perhaps in powered aircraft. The risk of collision between gliders of similar flying characteristics would be negligible. The maximum error in E.T.A. should not exceed five minutes either way. On nearing the objective, height would be lost as rapidly as possible in order to shorten the period passed within range of ground defences.

The disadvantages of releasing a long distance from the objective are:- good visibility is required, which aids the defences; greater responsibility is placed on the glider pilot, who probably casts off out of sight of the general landing area and must navigate under more difficult conditions than the navigator of a multi-seater tug. (To carry an additional navigator in each glider would reduce the numbers available for skilled military tasks on landing.) Once released from tow, the glider cannot outclimb bad weather, or make long detours to avoid it.

(b) Towing, possibly above or in cloud cover, to a release point from which the general landing area can be identified.

This method greatly simplifies the duties of the glider pilot, but involves greater risk for the tug, a longer vulnerable period on tow, and possible loss of surprise. It would be risky if attempted against any considerable fighter opposition.

> (c) Towing at low altitude to the immediate vicinity of the landing ground, to obtain surprise for at least a part of the force, and to make R.D.F. detection and A.A. and fighter attack more difficult. This method demands accurate judgment of the moment for the Germans on the Continent, provided the objective within the range of our fighter escorts and allows avoidance of the areas of heavy Flak, airborne attack is certainly possible in daylight without sustaining heavy casualties. But to reach an objective well inland and beyond our effective fighter range would be a hazardous operation.

[. . .]

92. The guns of bomber tugs could defend a formation but such guns as could be mounted on the gliders themselves could hardly be formidable against fighters, It seems inevitable that a gilder formation on tow must operate by night, in cloud cover, or with a strong "fighter umbrella". Fighters, if used as tugs, would be available for defence after the release.

93. Enemy fighters attacking a glider formation would themselves be highly vulnerable to attack by defending fighters, since the former must be flown comparatively slowly to attack effectively, and their manoeuvres should not be difficult to foresee. Defence by a fighter screen would force any attacking fighters to fly at higher speeds than are suitable for attacking gliders, or to deal with the defending fighters first.

Loss of Range

94. A free glider should be able to take reasonable evasive action against a single fighter, although it would be difficult to cope with two simultaneously. But evasive action is limited in time, owing to the extra loss of height, especially if the flaps are used. On trials the loss of range during continuous evasive action by a free glider has been between 25% and 40%. If the glider could be forced to land short of the objective, the purpose of the attack would have been achieved. Ample height margin is therefore needed if air attack is considered at all likely.

Landing

95. An airborne striking force must be highly concentrated in time and space. If a single aerodrome did not offer sufficient capacity, the extension of the landing area by the use of fields would be necessary, and would greatly reduce the total landing time. Probably no more than 3,000 troops per hour could be put down on an aerodrome. Few fields are so obstructed as to make glider landings impossible, if damage to the glider is accepted providing the

crew are uninjured, and especially if parachute troops have prepared the ground. The gliders themselves must be looked upon as "expendable stores" in the majority of operations in which they will be used, although this is very far from the truth in the case of pilots and crews.

96. Glider pilots might not all land at specific points in a surprise mass attack; large zones could be indicated in which the majority could land according to the conditions met. Pilots might be instructed to land in groups of about 7 or 10 aircraft. They would be familiarised with the main features by means of air-photographs and models. In the selection of the correct tactical landing point, the gilder pilot might require the assistance of the commander of the troops in the glider, who must be fully proficient in map-reading from aircraft. The troops should be able to fulfil their military rules from whatever starting point within the area the pilot was able to select, probably acting as independent units until an advanced stage of the battle.

97. Although the ground defences may have been forced to reveal their positions by dive-bombing, and put out of action before the landing of the airborne force, the enemy must be considered intelligent enough, if he suspects the intention, to order a proportion of the ground defences to hold their fire, or to make use of dummies and of mobile defences constantly changed.

98. The glider pilot should mistrust large and apparently unobstructed fields occurring within a generally obstructed area. If the enemy considers airborne attack likely, he will hardly have overlooked the opportunity of trapping the attacking force by leaving a few areas without visible obstructions, which would prove on landing either to have hidden obstructions or to be covered by machine guns, or even armoured vehicles, which last could be deadly to an airborne force directly after landing.

99. If good cover existed on the margin of the landing area, the pilot might well aim to end his landing run close to this cover even at some risk of collision with the boundary. If the glider came to rest near the middle of a field, the crew would be exposed on all sides whilst deplaning and assembling, and the glider would form an obstruction to the landing area.

100. But gliders would not normally be landed within range of immediate opposition. The German glider operations in Crete demonstrated that landings amongst highly organised defences are very costly.

101. If the general landing area were foreseen by the defenders, smoke screens might be laid over it. To land through such a smoke-screen could be a very risky operation. Conversely, smoke-screens might be laid by the attacking force to cover their approach, landing and assembly, perhaps incidentally providing a landmark and a wind indicator. A known defence position might be blinded in this way, by laying a smoke screen directly in front of it. Several

smoke grenades and candles exist for ground action, and in addition the following three types of smoke may be used to cover landing : -

    (a) Smoke ejected from containers carried in aircraft. By this means a really good smoke curtain can be lain at high speed, and its depth depends only on the number of aircraft used. Three aircraft, flying one above the other and echeloned slightly back from the lowest, can lay a very good continuous curtain 400 feet from ground level. The danger of this method is the vulnerability of the leading aircraft, but it will appear suddenly and only for a short time. Gliders and parachutists can land unseen behind this curtain.

    (b) White phosphorus Bombs. These are very useful for making the end or corners of a required smoke screen as a guide to smoke-laying aircraft.

    (c) Ordinary Smoke Candles. These can be dropped in large numbers from aircraft to form a smoke screen very quickly, perhaps to cover the approach of smoke-laying aircraft.

Duties of the Pilot after Landing

102. Glider-borne troops should arrive on the ground ready to go into action immediately. The pilot, whether Army or R.A.F, must take his part. Although he must be in command of the aircraft whilst at the base aerodrome and whilst in the air, he will not normally act as section leader after leading. To qualify to do he would have to train with the section throughout, which his flying training would hardly allow and he would then be restricted to flying with that section only. But he could very well be trained for special duties such as:-

    Liaison Duties.

    Marking and clearing landing grounds.

    Defence of landing grounds.

    Rear link wireless communications,

    Organisation of supply dumps.

    Organisation of A.A.

103. These tasks are in addition to the urgent necessity of killing the maximum number of the enemy and being able to look after himself in the battle. He should have some experience of guerrilla warfare (which is not merely haphazard fighting) and should be expert in the use of weapons.

104. He should be practical in memorising written orders and working with unmarked maps. In all German airborne operations to date a great amount of information has been gained from captured maps and orders. Airborne operations will be carried out in close co-operation with, but in advance of, other formations and services. It is imperative, therefore, that no

The component parts of an Airspeed Horsa before assembly.

marked maps or orders should be carried by Airborne troops from which the enemy could deduce the objectives or scope of the operation as a whole.

105.   In the first phase of an operation which was strongly opposed, there would probably be no assembly beyond groups of company strength. Units must be ready to act independently. Full organisation could only be expected in a later phase of the battle unless opposition were slight. The Crete campaign shows that rapid disorganisation sets in if airborne troops are not prepared for independent action in small units. An airborne force might be required to operate up to 500 miles from its base aerodromes, in the first instance against moderate resistance consisting of small arms fire, though subsequently it might have to meet attack by armoured fighting vehicles. Even after the assembly of its various units, it must be prepared to be self-contained up to a period of at least three days, and in certain circumstances might be isolated for long periods and might have to depend on airborne supply for its maintenance.

CHAPTER 4
AMPHIBIOUS ASSAULT

The amphibious assault phase of D-Day was the true test of all the planning and preparation. The first hours were critical. If the assault troops could not establish themselves on the beach, hold off counter-attacks, and push out beyond the sandy kill zones, the whole enterprise would fail.

The first manual in this chapter is *Ship to Shore Movement* (1943). This large US Navy work explained the intricacies of organisation and maritime skill required to take troops from sea to beach. For the US troops on D-Day, the practicalities of getting into the various landing craft (the characteristics of these craft are listed below) and moving to shore were relatively simple compared to what faced them on the beaches themselves. At Utah Beach, soldiers of the US 8th Infantry Regiment, 4th Infantry Division, confronted troops of the 919th Grenadier Regiment, the US troops supported by follow-up forces of 28 Sherman DD amphibious tanks and various combat engineer units. Although the American troops were landed in the wrong location – an effect of offshore currents that actually worked in their favour, as the new landing zone was less well-defended – by 0900 hours the troops were pushing inland, and by midday they had successfully landed 21,000 troops for only 197 casualties. The Utah forces were able to push inland to link up with troops from the 82nd and 101st Airborne Divisions. Just to the east of Utah beach, 200 men of the 2nd Ranger Battalion also climbed, took and defended the Pointe du Hoc headland, in an audacious action that involved the US Rangers scaling a 100ft-high cliff with ropes, grappling hooks and ladders.

The next beach landing to the east, Omaha Beach, stands out as the bloody landmark of the D-Day. Heavily defended by troops of the 352nd Infantry Division, Omaha Beach largely escaped the air bombardment – the bombs were dropped wide to avoid accidental strikes on naval forces – plus the German troops enjoyed high defensive bluffs overlooking wide, flat beaches, with their artillery and mortar positions behind mostly protected from the preparatory naval bombardment. Furthermore, the bulk of the DD tanks (27 out of 32) were swamped and sank offshore, while many of the landing craft beached on sandbars, forcing the troops to wade long distances ashore under murderous machine gun and artillery cross-fire.

The result was a near massacre, with the men of the 1st and 29th Infantry Divisions taking 2,000 casualties in a matter of hours. For a time, it looked as if the assault might fail here, but supporting naval gunfire from US destroyers and a tenacious advance up the beach's gulleys meant that by noon the German grip was eventually starting to loosen. Omaha Beach was eventually secured, but it took a hard day of bloody fighting, and the Allies were grateful that such an experience was not repeated on all the beaches.

Ship to Shore Movement (1943)

Chapter I.
General

101. Transbports and cargo ships.—

    a. In this pamphlet naval vessels which have been specially converted for transportation and landing of assault troops (Army or Marine Corps) will be referred to as "combat unit loaded transports" in order to differentiate them from other naval transports.

    b. Combat unit loaded transports (APA's) and combat unit loaded cargo ships (AKA's) are normally assigned to the Amphibious Forces, United States Fleet.

102. **Purpose.**—APA's and AKA's are designed to furnish transportation to assault troops and their equipment and to disembark them on hostile shores in the face of enemy resistance in the least possible time.

103. **Troop personnel usually assigned to combat unit loaded transports.—**

    a. Troop personnel usually assigned to a combat unit loaded transport will consist of a battalion of infantry with reinforcing units suitable for the accomplishment of a given task. Reinforcing units usually consist of artillery, tanks, antiaircraft weapons, antitank weapons, shore party, medical unit, motor transport unit.

    b. The transport division of several APA's and one or two AKA's should normally carry a reinforced regiment plus a proportion of division troops.

104. **Landing boats.**—As used herein, the term "landing boats" includes all craft designed for landing operations which are ship-borne. The term "landing craft" is used for all craft designed for landing operations which are less than 200 feet in length and *not* ship-borne.

Troops in an LCVP landing craft approach Omaha Beach on 6 June 1944.

Chapter II
Characteristics of Landing Boats

201. **Characteristics table.**—A table of characteristics will be found on the following pages. Paragraph 202 contains data on fuel consumption.

[. . .]

Chapter III
Debarkation

301. **General.**—The ship-to-shore movement covering the planning and execution of the movement of troops from the beginning of their debarkation from transports until they are landed on the beach is well covered in chapter IV of FTP 167. This chapter is concerned with the task organization composed of the landing boats in which the landing force is to move ashore in assault. The following instructions are intended to supplement FTP 167, with which all persons connected with the ship-to-shore movement must be familiar.

302. **Battle condition.**—

    a. Upon approaching the transport area all APA's and AKA's will go to general quarters. When the transport area is reached, set Condition One ABLE for the debarkation.

    b. Condition One ABLE (1A) is that condition of readiness in APA's and AKA's when all stations are fully manned for debarkation and unloading while at the same time the vessel is maintained in Condition One, insofar as available personnel permit. Services of the embarked troops will be made available to augment the ship's company, not to interfere with debarkation schedules.

303. **Transport area positions.**—A position in the transport area is assigned each transport and cargo vessel. Upon arrival at designated positions, transports and cargo vessels will anchor or lie to underway depending on wind and sea conditions prevailing at the time.

304. **Boat assignments.**—

a. It is the duty of the commander of the transports in a task group to furnish his corresponding troop commander with a boat availability table. This should indicated clearly which boats can be rail-loaded.

b. If it can be accomplished, the dispatching of boats to another transport should be limited to an adjacent vessel under conditions of reduced visibility.

c. If it can be accomplished, it is sound practice for a transport carrying a reserve battalion, to retain its boats for instant use by that battalion, augmented as required from the transport carrying the regimental headquarters.

d. Experience has indicated that the average APA and AKA paired have sufficient boats for landing a reinforced battalion in assault. After providing for two assault battalions in this manner, the normal transport division would therefore rely on the two remaining APA's for prompt landing of the reserve battalion.

305. **Lowering boats.**—

a. Upon arrival at designated points in the transport area, APA's are stopped and, when directed, all boats are put over as expeditiously as possible. Sea conditions permitting, this should be by simultaneous lowering on both sides. If sea conditions are such as to require a lee, port boats will be lowered first. As a matter of policy, vessels which can lower tank lighters and heavy equipment from but one side will use the starboard side for this operation.

b. Those vessels equipped with suitable davits and landing craft approved for lowering in loaded condition will habitually debark troops by lowering loaded from the rail.

c. The purpose of loading at the rail and lowering loaded is to shorten the debarkation time. This purpose will be defeated unless all measures for coordination and speed are carefully undertaken. Troops and equipment of the first boats to be lowered from the multiple bank davits may, when desirable, be loaded while the transports are

TABLE OF CHARACTERISTICS

Notes: "Speed" is with normal load, average sea. "Endurance" is at full speed. "Weight" is light unless otherwise noted. "Length" is O.A. unless otherwise noted.

Type A	Desig. letter B	Capacity C	Draft D	Weight E	Armor F	Arma-ment G	Speed (miles per hour) H	Endurance (miles) I	Length J	Beam K	Crew L
				Pounds							
1. Landing craft, rubber (small)	LCR(S)	7 troops		210	None	None			12 feet, 5 inches	5 feet, 8 inches	None
2. Landing craft, rubber (large)	LCR(L)	10 troops		¹320	None	1 .30 caliber machine gun	4-5 with 9½ horse power out board motor.		16 feet	8 feet	Do.
3. Landing craft, personnel (plastic)	LCP(P)	13 troops	10 inches	1,400	None	None	20		32 feet	7 feet, 10 inches	
4. Landing craft personnel (large)	LCP(L)	30-36 troops; or 6,700-8,100 pounds cargo (depending on fuel load)	3 feet	12,500	3 transverse bulk heads, ¼-inch	2 .30 caliber machine guns	10	80 or 200	36 feet	10 feet, 8 inches	3

TABLE OF CHARACTERISTICS

5. Landing craft, personnel (ramp)	LCP(R)	30–36 troops; or 6,700–8,100 pounds cargo (depending on fuel load).	3 feet	12,500	3 transverse bulk heads, ¼-inch	2 .30 caliber machine guns	10	80 or 200	36 feet	10 feet, 8 inches	3
6. Landing craft, vehicle-personnel	LCVP	36 troops or 1.1-ton truck of 8,100 pounds cargo (hold 18feet, 3 inches × 6 feet, 3 inches)	3 feet, 2 inches	17,850	¼ sides and ramp	2 .30 caliber machine guns	10	100	36 feet, 4 inches	10 feet, 9 inches	4
7. Landing craft, vehicle	LCV	36 troops or, 1.1-ton truck, or, 10,000 pounds cargo (hold 18 feet, 5 inches × 6 feet 3 inches)	3 feet	13,000	None	None	10	80 or 200	36 feet, 4 inches	10 feet, 9½ inches	3
8. Landing craft control	LCC	Crew only	4 feet	50,000	¼ inch bridge	3 twin .50 caliber machine guns	15 knots	500	56 feet	15 feet	

TABLE OF CHARACTERISTICS

				20,000	¼ inch	2 .50 caliber, 3.30 caliber machine guns	16	60	36 feet, 6 inches	10 feet, 9 inches	6
				Longtons							
9. Landing craft support (small)	LSC(S)	3 or 4 persons in addition to crew and gunners	3 feet								
10. Landing craft mechanized, Mark II	LCM(2)	1 light (13½-ton) tank; or, 30,000-pound cargo; or 100 troops	3 feet	25	Control station, ½ inch	2 .50 caliber machine guns	8.5	75	45 feet	14 feet	4
11. Landing craft,[2] mechanized, Mark III	LCM(3)	1 medium (30-ton) tank; or 60,000-pound cargo or 120 troops. (Cargo area 32 feet x 9 feet 7 inches, average)	3 feet 6 inches	22	Control station, ¼ inch	2 .50 caliber machine guns	10	125	50 feet	14 feet	4
12. Landing craft tank, Mark V	LCT(5)	3 heavy (50-ton) tanks; or 5 medium (30-ton) tanks	3 feet 1 inch fwd., 3 feet 9 inches	124	Control station, ¼ inch	2 20-mm. guns	10	500	108 feet, O.A.; 105 B.P.	32 feet	1 officer, 10 enlisted

TABLE OF CHARACTERISTICS

13. Landing craft, infantry (large)	LCI(L)	192 troops or 75 tons cargo	2 feet 6 inches fwd., 4 feet 6 inches aft	216	¼ inch sides fwd., ⅜ bridge shield	4 20-mm. guns	17 knots	4,000 (ocean) (500 landing)	158 feet 4 inches O.A.	23 feet 3 inches	2 officers, 21 enlisted
14. Landing ship, dock	LSD	195 troops and 14 LCM(3) loaded (or 3 LCT (5) loaded) and 10 trucks on deck; or 1,500 longs tons cargo	14 feet 6 inches	5,850	Splinter	1 3"/.50 gun; 8.20-mm. guns	16 knots	8,000 at 15 knots	457 feet 9 inches	72 feet	200
15. Landing ship, tank	LST	186 troops and 10 heavy (50-ton) or 20 medium (30-ton) tanks or 39 light tanks (13-ton)	3 feet fwd., 9 feet 4 inches aft	1,412	do	6 20-mm. guns	11 knots	5,000	328 feet	50 feet	7 officers, 57 enlisted

1. Without motor.
2. Higgins Type.

still underway so that the lowering of this group may commence immediately on arrival in the transport area. Troops in the first boats so lowered should include, if possible, all those intended for the first wave. Subsequent boats lowered from the multiple bank davits should likewise be preloaded and include troops and equipment which follow in normal sequence the order of landing. Arrival in the transport area should be so timed as to ensure the minimum interval between the commencement of lowering boats and arrival at the beach at the prescribed H-hour, in accordance with the landing force commander's plan of attack. These are matters of arrangement between the appropriate naval and military commanders but smart execution by transport personnel of the loading and lowering is essential in order to meet the agreed time schedule with the minimum interval. Attention is directed to the necessity for troop units to be on station and in all respects prepared for immediate debarkation when assigned landing boats are ready. In some cases it may be desirable to retard the unloading of the troops (as, for instance, while heavy equipment is being unloaded to accompany the assault troops) in order to shorten the time spent in boats on the water.

d. *Stations for rail-loaded davit boats.*—

    a. Troops assigned to a davit boat will assemble inboard of the boat, when possible.

    b. Ladders or gangplanks must be provided as necessary to expedite the loading of boats.

e. Immediately on being lowered, loaded boats will proceed to the rendezvous area where they will join up by boat divisions and form the landing waves.

f. *Lowering details.*—Each APA and AKA will organize permanent details for lowering all landing craft..

306. Loading alongside.—

a. *Boat assembly areas.*—As soon as *unloaded* boats are in the water, they proceed to the boat assembly areas. The location of these areas is as follows:

    1. *When debarking simultaneously from both sides.*—For LCP, LCV, and LCVP, two boat assembly areas, one on each quarter at 250 yards distance. These boats take station in the area corresponding to the side from which they were lowered, either from the parent or another vessel. For LCM and any larger craft assigned, astern, clear of the quarter assembly areas but within effective visual signal distance.

2. *When debarking from one side only.*—For LCP, LCV and LCVP, one assembly area 250 yards distant on the starboard quarter. For LCM, one assembly area on the starboard beam. Any larger craft assigned, astern.

b. Boats will circle at reduced speed in the following directions:

1. Boats on starboard quarter and astern will circle in a clockwise direction while waiting to be called alongside.

2. Boats on the port quarter will circle in a counterclockwise direction while waiting to be called alongside.

3. Boats on the starboard beam will circle in a counterclockwise direction.

c. An officer will be designated to take charge of the assembly circles. He will see that assembly circles are properly formed and maintained and that signals received from the ship's debarkation officer are promptly obeyed.

d. All boats in the assembly areas will maintain a sharp watch on the after signal station for signals to come alongside.

e. When boats from other vessels are assigned to an APA, they will join the appropriate assembly areas and assume automatically the status of the parent transport's own boats. Any boat officer from other vessels will act only as assistants to the assault wave commanders.

f. *Debarkation stations.*—Troops (other than those lowered in boats) debark by debarkation nets over the side of the ship at debarkation stations. Each APA should have not less than four debarkation stations on each side. Each AKA should have not less than two per side. Debarkation stations are designated by number and color from forward to aft as follows:

	Starboard	Port	Color
Debarkation station	No. 1	No. 2	Red.
Do	No. 3	No. 4	White.
Do	No. 5	No. 6	Blue.
Do	No. 7	No. 8	Yellow.
Do	No. 9	No. 10	Green.

g. The following considerations govern the location and rigging of debarkation stations.

1. Deck adjacent to station as spacious and free of obstructions as possible to facilitate standing-by and passage of troops over the side.

2. Ship's side to be approximately vertical and without excessive flare such as exists under the bow or counter.

3. Stations should be separated as necessary in order that routes for troops moving from "boat load" assembling places below decks do not cross.

4. Afford proper securings for the nets.

5. Provide handrail for the troops to grasp when climbing on the net.

6. Sea painters and boat lines should be provided for each station.

7. The foot of the cargo net should extend to one foot below the load water line.

8. The head of the debarkation net should be neatly secured at the edge of the deck without bulkiness, doubling or folding.

9. Nets should be held spread by 4x4 beams lashed in place between the net and the side of the ship. The lowest spreader should be about seven feet above the foot of the net. Additional spreaders should be inserted as necessary to maintain the net at uniform width throughout its length.

10. Two lines to the lower corners of the debarkation net, tended on deck, will facilitate debarkation and prevent the fouling of boat's propellers. This is accomplished by raising the bottom of nets prior to arrival and departure of boats.

h. The location of stations for the unloading of vehicles and cargo will be governed by the following factors:

1. Station must be located adjacent to hatches.

2. The radius of the cargo booms.

3. Vehicles crews must debark at their loading stations.

i. *Loading boats.*—

1. As long as any man is on the net, either debarking or embarking, the bottom end of the net will be tended in the boat by the boat crew or troops and the net be kept free of slack as the boat rises or falls with the sea, in order to form a ladder direct from the ship's deck to the bottom of the boat.

2. In addition to the nets rigged at the debarkation stations, a net or ladder will be rigged abeam of each hatch from which troop equipment and supplies are to be discharged. This net or ladder will provide a means of debarkation for working parties handling equipment or supplies in the boat.

307. **Debarkation stations operating instructions.—**

    a. Special details.—

        1. A ship's officer, trained as debarkation officer, will be stationed on the bridge. He will be in general charge of the unloading and his primary task is to have the proper type of boat at a debarkation station ready for loading of boat when required. He is furnished by the commanding officer of the embarked battalion, a debarkation schedule, which indicates what type boat is to be at debarkation station at any time. He also keeps a check-off list of boats loaded and dispatched.

        2. A ship's officer will be stationed at the after signal station which is so located as to be clearly visible to all boats in the assembly areas. His duty is to order boats from the assembly areas to debarkation stations.

        3. A ship's officer or qualified petty officer and a troop officer will be stationed at each debarkation station. [. . .] the ship's officer or petty officer is responsible for keeping the debarkation officer informed of the following:

        When ready for a boat.

        When boat is almost loaded.

        When the loaded boat departs and its number.

        4. An enlisted man trained in debarkation signals will be stationed at each debarkation station, and a signalman at the after signal station.

        5. A radioman who is in communication with the boat group commander and assistant boat group commander will be stationed with the debarkation officer.

        6. The debarkation officer will maintain direct communication with the after signal station and with each debarkation station.

    *b. Calling alongside.—*The following designating letters and numbers shall be used for calling the various types of boats alongside:

LCP(L)	Love.
LCP(R)	Roger.
LCV	Victor.
LCVP	Peter.
LCS(S)	Sugar.
LCC	Charlie.
LCM(2)	Two flag.
LCM(3)	Three flag.
LCT and LVT(A)	Zebra.

c. Equipment.—

    1. At each debarkation station:

        a. A flag (semaphore size) and a flashlight of the color assigned to the debarkation station.

        b. A sound-powered telephone connected with the debarkation officer and the after signal station.

    2. At the after signal station:

        a. A set of flags corresponding to the flags designating types of landing boats (should be size No. 6 or larger).

        b. A set of flags with colors corresponding to the colors of the debarkation stations (size No. 6 or larger).

        c. A set of colored lights with colors corresponding to the colors of the debarkation stations.

        d. A sound-powered telephone connected with the debarkation officer and each debarkation station.

        e. When debarking from both sides *two* sets of signaling apparatus will be provided.

    3. At the debarkation officer's station:

        a. A portable loud speaker with which to communicate directly with boats alongside or lying to close aboard.

        b. Sound-powered telephone connected with the after signal station and with each debarkation station.

    4. The intensity of lights will be the minimum necessary to accomplish their purpose.

d. Debarkation system in operation.—

    1. By day, landing boats are called alongside by the after signal station on orders from the debarkation officer by the use of flags. For example: Station No. 5 informs the debarkation officer that the boat alongside that station is almost loaded. The debarkation officer looks at his list and sees that the next boat required at Station No. 5 is an LCP(R). He then directs the after signal station to send and LCP(R) to No. 5 (Blue) debarkation station. The after Signal Station displays a ROGER flag and a BLUE flag on the starboard side. The nearest LCP(R) in the corresponding assembly area leaves the circle and goes alongside No. 5 debarkation station when clear.

2. During darkness, the after signal station calls boats alongside by making on the appropriate side the Morse symbol corresponding to the type of boat desired, using the colored light corresponding to the color of the station at which the craft is desired. For example: In the case cited in the above paragraph, the after signal station would make ROGER with a blue colored light on the starboard side indication that an LCP(R) was desired at No. 5 (BLUE) station.

3. Larger vessels, such as LST's, LCI(L) and LCT(5), will be ordered to debarkation stations by flashing light. These craft will be called individually.

308. **Boat identification.**—A designated member of each boat load of debarking troops carries with him into the boat a board, provided by the APA, on which has been painted the designated number of the boat. This board will be displayed prominently during the loading and while in the boat. The number indicates two things, the boat division and the boat number in that boat division. The first digit or digits indicates the boat division and the last digit the boat number within the boat division. The lowest numbered boat within the boat division indicates the boat division commander. Each coxswain is also furnished a copy of the landing diagram showing the number of the wave in which he belongs and his position in that wave.

309. **Stadiameter.**—In order to ensure proper distances between landing craft are maintained during ship to shore movements, each boat will be provided with a stadiameter of design as indicated in figure 19, FTP 167.

Figure 19. Use of a stadiameter

310. **Unloading vehicles and equipment.—**

    a. *Equipment.—*

        1. Troop equipment, other than individual equipment, will be loaded in the rail-loaded boats before arrival in the transport area.

        2. In loading boats in the water, equipment will be loaded in the boat before the troops embark. The boat crew, and such troops as necessary, will be in the boat to handle equipment as it is lowered into the boat.

    b. *Vehicles.—*

        1. Vehicles must be loaded with great care to insure that they are headed toward the bow of the boat.

        2. Crews of vehicles will embark in the boats immediately before the vehicles are loaded. These crews, with the aid of the boat crew, will insure proper loading.

    If possible, a vehicle that is not self-propelled will be loaded with the vehicle furnishing its motive power.

311. **Rendezvous areas.—**

    a. Immediately on being loaded, boats will proceed to the rendezvous area.

    b. *Definition.*—A rendezvous area is an area designated for the assembly of loaded boat waves preparatory to their departure for the line of departure.

    c. *Location.—*

        1. The rendezvous area is located between 500 and 1,500 yards (depending upon the visibility) from the APA on the line between the APA and the center of the line of departure. The rendezvous area is a fixed position.

        2. The rendezvous area is marked by the presence of the control vessel which is responsible for the correct location of this area.

        3. The control vessel will, if possible, stay on the line between the APA and the center of the line of departure with its bow headed toward the center of the line of departure. By observing the control vessel, boats in the rendezvous area can determine the direction to the center of the line of departure and can also check the compass course.

        4. The formation of waves in the rendezvous area will be prescribed by commander transport group according to the attending circumstances.

d. *Operating instructions.—*

1. Coxswains of loaded boats will obtain the position of the control vessel from the debarkation station while being loaded.

2. Waves will assemble in the rendezvous area under the direction of the wave commanders. Odd numbered waves will circle *slowly* in a clockwise direction while even numbered waves will circle in a counterclockwise direction.

312. Movement from the rendezvous area to the line of departure.—

a. *During daylight in good visibility.—*

1. The first wave follows the control vessel when that vessel leaves the rendezvous area for the line of departure. A deployed formation should be used.

2. The second and succeeding waves follow at the intervals between their designated times of landing on the beach.

3. Wave commanders are responsible for leading their waves from the rendezvous area at the correct time interval behind the wave preceding them.

4. A distance of at least 50 yards shall be kept between boats in a wave.

b. *During darkness or poor visibility.—*

1. Boat waves must proceed to the line of departure in a group, leading wave following closely the control vessel, in a formation suitable to conditions of visibility. Waves will follow each other in their numerical order.

2. Wave commanders are responsible for their waves and will not lose sight of the control vessel or the wave ahead, if not in the first wave.

3. The interval between waves will be determined by the visibility. The maximum interval practicable will be maintained.

4. Distances between individual boats in a wave will be determined by the visibility but all units will keep closed up enough to insure their seeing the unit ahead of them at all times.

c. *Movements on arrival at the line of departure.—*

1. During daylight, waves will take assault formation just prior to arrival at the line of departure and will start for the beach on signal by the control vessel.

2. During darkness, waves will form circles on a line to seaward of the control vessel on the beach-control vessel axis. The first

US troops wade ashore under German gunfire on D-Day.

waves takes the assault formation and proceeds to the beach on signal from the control vessel. As the first wave departs for the beach, the second wave moves in close to the control vessel. As the second wave leaves, the third wave moves up and so on.

3. To minimize the danger for aerial bombing or strafing, shell fire from the beach or from enemy surface craft, waves and boats in waves, must be kept separated and staggered as much as possible. This is particularly important during periods of good visibility when the boat group is extremely vulnerable.

313. From the line of departure to the beach.—

a. Wave commanders will be particularly vigilant in keeping boats at the proper distances. There exists a very strong tendency to bunch and this must be overcome. Use the stadiameter.

b. Best speed consistent with maintaining the assault formation will be used in the dash to the beach.

c. Over the last 1,000 yards, individual boats use full speed.

314. Movements of landing craft subsequent to initial landing.—

a. *Retraction.*—Each boat must retract immediately after its load is on the beach.

b. *Return to the ship.*—

1. After retracting all boats will return to their assigned vessel unless otherwise directed.

2. At night, landing boats should take advantage of the control vessel, the traffic control boat, incoming waves and individual beach-bound boats, to find their way back to their ships.

3. Wave commanders will aid boats returning to their ships as much as possible but no attempt will be made to reform waves.

315. *Rules of the road for landing boats.*—

a. All coxswains of boats will have a working knowledge of the Rules of the Road as they apply to their boats.

b. The following general rules will be observed to avoid collisions between boats during an operation.

1. Boats will keep to the right in meeting.

2. Empty boats will keep clear of loaded boats by moving to the nearest flank except in the following instances when it becomes the loaded boat's duty to keep clear:

While an empty boat in retraction still has its bow toward the beach.

While an empty boat is towing another boat.

3. A beach-bound assault wave shall have the right of way over all other boats which will be careful not to interfere in any manner.

316. **Transport identification.**—If the attack force commander prescribes transport identification, the following system will be used. When debarkation commences, each transport (APA) will display its transport number in the form of a colored panel and a colored signal light will be used in conjunction with the panel display. This panel may be a sectional wooden panel, if deck space permits, or colored fabric rigged awning-fashion. Colored oilcloth should be used if available because of its light-reflecting properties. Transports on which an initial assault battalion of infantry is embarked will display the number of the ship in color of the beach on which the embarked battalion is to land. All transports not landing an initial assault battalion will display white numbers. Colored numbers will be on a white background, white numbers on a black background.

317. **Boat group identification for aviation.**—Each boat group will display, in each boat of its leading wave, a panel of the color of the beach at which the boat group has been ordered to land. A signal light of the same color will be used in conjunction with the panel display. The panel will be of rectangular form 8 feet long and 4 feet wide. The panel will be made of fabric and will be displayed over the engine hood or other conspicuous part of the boat, and the heads of troops so as to be clearly visible to aircraft. Colored oilcloth is recommended for the reasons stated in paragraph 316. This panel

will be furnished by the troops embarked in the boats of the leading wave. In the event that troops are to be landed on two or more beaches of the same color the boat group will identify itself to the aircraft by indicating the number of the beach by signaling with appropriate colored signal light.

318. **Guide plane identification.**—Each guide plane and boat group will be provided by the Navy with a colored signal lamp. To establish and maintain communication with the boat group, the guide plane will employ the color of the beach toward which it is to guide the designated boat group.

As stated below in the *Manual of Combined Operations*, 'The army's principal task is, with the assistance of the navy and the air force, to establish a footing in enemy territory despite any opposition offered to the landing operations.' The considerations in how to achieve this are explained in detail below, including the physical nature of the landing zone, the hour of the day and the phases of assault.

Landings on the three British beaches began a little later than those at the American sites, to take account for differences in tidal patterns. At Gold Beach, British infantry of the 50th Infantry Division and Royal Marines, supported by DD tanks of 8th Armoured Brigade, faced a testing network of strongpoints and well-defended coastal buildings, often requiring the support of close-in naval gunfire, tanks or Royal Engineer demolition vehicles to breach. A breakout was eventually accomplished with around 1,000 casualties, but the British troops faced heavy counter-attacks from the 21st Panzer Division.

The adjacent Juno Beach was mainly the remit of the 3rd Canadian Infantry Division and the 2nd Canadian Armoured Brigade. Juno was the scene of some especially heavy fighting, as like Omaha the German defences had not been adequately suppressed, and the beach and surrounding area became especially congested, causing sluggish movement. Even as the Canadian soldiers eventually pushed inland, they came across numerous dogged German positions, which by the end of the day had inflicted more than 960 Canadian casualties.

Sword Beach was the easternmost of the landing beaches, and assaulted principally by the British 3rd Infantry Division and 27th Armoured Brigade. As at Juno, beach congestion was a major problem, made worse by the presence of large numbers of anti-tank mines. Nevertheless, with the support of 21 DD tanks the British (and some Free French) forces gained a lodgment, and began inching out of the landing zone inland towards Caen. The Sword units also received the counter-attack by the 21st Panzer Division, which was eventually beaten off although with high casualties – the troops at Sword suffered a total of about 1,000 casualties during the day.

Manual of Combined Operations (1938)

PART V
LANDINGS ON HOSTILE SHORES
CHAPTER 18
LANDINGS ON HOSTILE SHORES IN GENERAL

Types of Landing Operations

1. Operations in which landings in enemy territory play the principal part may be classified as follows:

(i) Operations with a destructive or diversionary object which can be achieved within a short time and followed by re-embarkation. These are commonly known as raids.

(ii) Operations involving the subsequent maintenance ashore of the force landed. Such operations may be undertaken with a variety of objects and consequently on widely differing scales. There are, however, two main types of such operations—

(*a*) Operations where the full mobility of the force landed is not required. Thus the object may be the establishment of a fleet or air base at, or in the immediate vicinity of, the point of landing. It may be that the force carrying out the original assault is sufficient to complete the capture of the base and thereafter to render it secure from land attack, or it may be necessary to land considerable reinforcements after the assaulting force has made good the landing. In this type of operation the function of the land forces which have carried out the assault on the beaches becomes a purely defensive one once they have attained positions in which they can ensure the security of the final objective. A full scale of transport and equipment is not, therefore, necessaryand the subsequent problem of maintenance iscorrespondingly easier.

(*b*) Operations where the force landed is required to be fully mobile. Thus the object may be to use the seized territory as a base for the offensive operations of the army or to establish an air base a considerable distance inland. In these cases the force carrying out the original assault acts as a covering force for the landing of the main body. Important considerations after the assaulting force is established in a covering position are not only the actual landing of the main body but the way in which the harbours, coasts, and beaches that have been seized can be made an adequate base for the maintenance of the whole force when acting on the offensive.

(iii) Offensive operations similar to the above but in which the landing forces are intended to join hands with forces already operating in the vicinity, making use of the latter's lines of communication. In this type of operation the use of the landing beaches as supply bases on an extensive scale is therefore not required. As soon as the landing has been made good all attention can be concentrated on landing the main body, with no more supply organization than is needed to sustain it until it is able to use the existing land lines of communication.

(iv) Operations with an offensive aim requiring time for its achievement but for which the forces needed are on so small a scale that they are of insufficient importance to attract heavy enemy air attack. In this case they can be maintained ashore through bases not equipped with a full scale of air defence.

2. It is on the type of operation as classified above that the strength, composition and equipment of the land forces taking part will chiefly depend. In each type, however, the phases with which the co-operation of the three Services is chiefly concerned (approach from seaward; landing the assaulting force; subsequent reinforcement and maintenance ashore) have many features in common whatever the nature and aim of the forces to be landed. The problems of landing on a hostile shore will therefore be considered in the main under a classification in accordance with these phases but paying attention to variations imposed on each phase by the type and eventual aim of the operation as a whole.

The Nature of the Military Problem

3. The army's principal task is, with the assistance of the navy and the air force, to establish a footing in enemy territory despite any opposition offered to the landing operations. As regards the nature of this opposition, a degree of naval security sufficient to overcome interference with the ships of the expedition will also suffice to prevent naval opposition to the landing operations. The opposition to the landing that may be expected will therefore be either from land forces or air forces or both.

CHAPTER 22
LANDING THE ASSAULTING FORCE
Section 1—GENERAL CONSIDERATIONS
Three principal decisions—general consideration

1. The three principal decisions governing the operation of landing the assaulting force are:—

(i) The locality of the landing.

(ii) The strength and composition of the assaulting force

(iii) Whether the first assault is to be by day or night.

2. The locality of the landing and the strength of the assaulting force will depend primarily on the aim and nature of the operations as a whole. Within the limitations imposed by these conditions the first consideration will be the part which surprise may play in reducing the probable scale of opposition. If, by landing in an unexpected locality, a footing can be established with little opposition, this consideration may outweigh many physical difficulties

Royal Marine Commandos attached to 3rd Infantry Division move inland from Sword beach, 6 June 1944.

connected with the use of landing places not in themselves suitable. It may even be advisable to land at some distance from the objective and to accept the necessity for a long approach march and the consequent delay, if, by so doing, the uncertainties and possible heavy casualties of a landing in face of opposition can be avoided.

3. On the other hand a landing may have to be made on a part of the coast for the defence of which by land forces the enemy has made some preparation. Under these conditions a suitable locality for the landing will depend, subject to the general nature of the operation, partly on hydrographic and topographic factors and partly on the composition of the assaulting force and the task required of it. In addition to establishing itself ashore, the assaulting force may have to cover landing places, not necessarily those at which it was itself landed, from which it can be supplied and reinforced, and at which any forces required for further operations can be landed. The requirements of landing places for these subsequent operations are considered in Chapter 24. It will also be desirable for the covering position to include advanced landing grounds for aircraft.

4. The general nature of the military plan will sometimes make it advisable to land in several places sufficiently widely separated for the landings to be considered as distinct operations, each under the direction of an O.C.

Assaulting Force. Normally it would be intended that each of these landings should play a predetermined part in the subsequent operations; but the inevitable uncertainties of opposed landings may make it necessary to achieve the eventual aim through one or more successful landings, either re-embarking the forces at the others or maintaining them on the defensive. It may even be advisable to plan several landings with the primary intention of exploiting the most successful rather than of making eventual use of all.

Physical Factors affecting the Locality of the Landing

5. Subject, then, to the general nature of the operation, any sheltered anchorages or advanced landing grounds to be embraced by the covering position, and the superior claims of surprise, the following are the main factors that enter into the choice of a locality. When considering the effect of these physical factors, however, due weight must be given to the probability that the enemy will pay most attention to the easiest landing places.

    (i) Suitability of landing places for landing men, tanks, guns, M.T. vehicles, animals and stores, including the range of tide over which they are practicable.

    (ii) Distance of landing places from water navigable by the ships carrying the assaulting force and any ships that are required to provide supporting fire.

    (iii) Navigational considerations affecting the passage of landing craft between ships and shore.

    (iv) Nature of exits from the landing places to the country beyond.

    (v) Suitability of the country for employment of tanks.

    (vi) Suitability of the country for employment of naval covering fire.

    (vii) Suitability of the country for the establishment of a covering position.

    (viii) Existence of suitable areas for assembly positions, and dumps.

6. A sandy beach that shelves rapidly at all states of the tide and has a clear approach from seaward with deep water close inshore is the most suitable from the naval point of view. If these conditions can be combined with good exits and a low terrain in the neighbourhood of the beach, the major physical requirements for rapid landing of military forces will have been met.

Anti-submarine Defence

7. A further factor influencing the selection of the locality for a landing is the suitability of anchorages in the vicinity for anti-submarine defence. Defence of the expedition against submarine attack during the landing of the assaulting force must be ensured mainly by methods similar to those employed during the approach, *i.e.*, by the operations of destroyers and aircraft. The

The invasion fleet crosses the Channel, with barrage balloons anchored to the craft for anti-aircraft defence.

dangers of attack will, however, be increased when ships are stopped or anchored for the purpose of disembarking their forces; and whenever these operations are carried out by, or extended into, daylight, additional danger must be offset as far as possible by selecting anchorages the natural features of which will add to the difficulties of submarine attack.

Effect of Weather

8. An over-ruling factor in all landing operations is the state of the weather, considered in conjunction with the shelter afforded by land or shoals to the landing places and to the positions in which the forces are transferred from ships to landing craft. Landing on sand or shingle beaches will be impracticable in anything more than a moderate surf, and landing on a rocky foreshore will only be possible in smooth water. Similarly, reasonably smooth water will be required for transfer of troops, tanks, guns, M.T. vehicles, animals and stores from ships to landing craft.

9. Ideal conditions are those in which landing places and positions for transfer from ships to landing craft are sheltered from any probable wind and swell. In most cases, however, complete shelter is unlikely and some degree of reliance must be placed on favourable weather. This will entail a study of weather conditions in the locality in so far as they affect swell and onshore winds and in connection with the practicability of reliable forecasting.

10. In addition to the effect of weather on the actual landing operations, adverse weather may hamper air operations, and, if the success of the landing is likely to be seriously affected thereby, this aspect must be given consideration.

11. A further matter in which weather forecasting will play an important part is the use of smoke screens.

12. It will as a rule be necessary to make arrangements for modifying or postponing the operations in the event of the weather being more unfavourable than was expected.

Size and Composition of the Assaulting Force

13. The task of the assaulting force comprises two phases:—

(i) The capture of the landing places.

(ii) The advance to and capture of a covering position extent as is necessary to secure the next phase of the operation. Thus, this security may be required either for the supply and reinforcement of the assaulting force, the landing of a force intended to carry out further operations, or the re-embarkation of the assaulting force after achieving its object. Normally, therefore, the covering position should be such as will ensure the freedom of the landing places and the anchorages off them from ground-observed artillery fire.

14. The size of the assaulting force will depend on—

(i) The scale and the nature of the anticipated opposition.

(ii) The extent of the front on which the landing is to be carried out.

(iii) The extent of the covering position to be occupied by the force after landing and the topography of the country in the vicinity.

15. The assaulting force should be self-contained and capable of maintaining itself with a minimum of transport until such time as the beaches are sufficiently organized to allow reinforcement and normal maintenance to begin, or until such time as it re-embarks, according to the type of operation. Where the assaulting force is acting as a covering force for a main body to be disembarked subsequently, this period should be at least 48 hours. The assaulting force must also—

(i) Be capable of rapid manoeuvre.

(ii) Possess great fire power.

(iii) Be equipped for defence against low-flying aircraft.

(iv) Be free from all unnecessary impedimenta which would adversely affect a quick and easy landing.

16. To meet these requirements the assaulting force should consist primarily of infantry, tanks and close-support weapons which may or may not include some field artillery. 3·7-in. howitzers form a very valuable weapon in the earlier stages of a landing owing to the ease with which they can be transported ashore. They may be drawn from both naval and military sources.

17. The infantry should be as lightly equipped as possible, bearing in mind the task which confronts them. It will seldom be possible to land any quantity of transport during the operations for securing a covering position and it will therefore be necessary to cut down the scale of equipment with troops. All normal administrative arrangements must be reviewed and units must be prepared to fight with a minimum of transport. In the early stages this will probably best be achieved by forming a small pool for the force as a whole. The use of aircraft for dropping supplies by means of parachutes may also be advisable. Where the nature of the country is suitable, pedal cycles form a valuable means of rapid intercommunication and are easier to land than horses or any form of motor vehicle.

18. There will seldom be sufficient landing craft to land the whole assaulting force at once, and even if there are it will not usually be advisable to do so. For one thing, there may not be room at each point of landing to deploy all the forces destined for it; and for another, the difficulties of an initial landing are such that an adequate footing may not be gained at every point attacked and some part of the force must therefore be kept in hand to exploit success. Moreover, as in all forms of land warfare it is necessary to have some form of general reserve with which to influence the course of the battle.

19. The assaulting force is therefore divided into—

    (i) The first flight, whose duty is to capture and secure the landing places.

    (ii) The second and subsequent flights.

    (iii) The floating reserve.

Night or Day Landings

20. When it is intended to effect a landing despite the presence of enemy troops in the area of operations, complete surprise at the point of landing will as a rule only be possible by night. A night landing will also reduce the probability of air opposition. Night landings, however, suffer under certain disadvantages, viz.—

    (i) The difficulty of finding the intended landing places.

    (ii) The difficulty of co-ordinating the movements of landing craft intended for different landing places.

    (iii) The difficulty of advancing in the dark over unreconnoitred country, and hence the difficulty of exploiting success.

    (iv) Should serious opposition be encountered there will be more difficulty in overcoming it than by day, and it must be overcome without the assistance of naval gunfire or close-support air action.

    (v) Should air attacks develop, they will be more difficult to counter than by day.

21. In general, it may be said that, where the enemy has considerable forces in the area of operations, but where at the same time the choice of landing places is so wide that he cannot defend them all, a night landing will probably offer the best chance of success.

22. Conversely, should the choice of landing places be so restricted that the enemy, though lacking in total strength in the area, has been able to establish defences at each, the best way of overcoming those defences will be an exactly executed and accurately co-ordinated attack, carried out with the assistance of smoke and with the support of naval gunfire and air operations against ground targets. Such a landing must be made by day.

23. As the composition of the forces landing, type of landing craft employed, choice of landing places and general conduct of the operation will differ considerably between day and night landing these matters must be considered separately under those headings.

24 In order to derive full benefit from a night approach, while at the same time avoiding the disadvantages of a night landing, the landing may be timed to take place at or soon after dawn. Such an operation, though it may be assisted by darkness until shortly before the first flight land, is, however, essentially a daylight landing and will be considered in that category.

[...]

Section III—DAY LANDINGS

64. Though some degree of surprise will probably be essential for the success of a day landing, either strategical surprise or a partial tactical surprise obtained by a night approach, the conduct of the landing must be based on arrangements for overcoming opposition at the landing places. Ability to overcome this opposition will depend partly on the composition of the assaulting force and the type of craft employed in landing it, and partly on the support received from warships and aircraft.

65. The forms of opposition which may be encountered are:—

    (i) Machine gun, light machine gun and rifle fire.

    (ii) Fire from anti-tank guns and mobile artillery.

(iii) Anti-tank mines.

(iv) Under-water obstructions.

(v) Wire.

(vi) Gas contamination.

(vii) Low-flying aircraft attack—either machine gun, bomb, or gas-spray.

66. As the initial advance from the grounded landing craft will usually be the most difficult phase of the operation, and as the opposition of unlocated machine guns during this phase will be the most difficult to overcome, it will be advisable to include tanks in the first wave of the attack on the beaches. Tanks may also be the only means of destroying wire obstacles on the beaches. Consideration of ease of landing and handiness will usually call for the employment of light tanks on this duty. Where the country is suitable for their employment tanks of all natures may also be required subsequently for the advance to the covering position.

67. Machine guns may also be used by the enemy in an endeavour to prevent the assaulting force reaching the shore. The troops in the landing craft may be subjected to this fire as they approach the landing places, and they may be further menaced at this time by low-flying aircraft and by fire from anti-tank guns and artillery It will not be possible to incorporate in the landing craft the means for a complete resistance to all these forms of attack, but some protection will be needed against the most dangerous threat, viz.. machine gun fire.

Landing Craft

68. For a day landing it is therefore essential in the earlier stages that:—

(i) A proportion of the landing craft should be capable of carrying tanks.

(ii) The landing craft carrying men should be provided with protection against machine gun fire—including as much protection against fire from low-flying aircraft as is practicable.

69. The types of landing craft that may be available are given in Chapter 8. The only existing craft that can fulfil either of the above requirements for the earlier stages of a landing are motor landing craft and motor lighters, but the possibility of constructing special craft for a particular operation must not be overlooked.

70. A possible exception to the need of protection against machine guns lies in the employment of small fast craft which would be such difficult targets that machine gun fire against them would be comparatively ineffectual. The use of such craft in numbers would avoid one of the principal disadvantages

of motor landing craft and motor lighters, viz., that a large body of infantry debouching over a single brow presents a favourable target for enemy machine guns.

Choice of Localities for Landing

71. The choice of localities for landing, referred to above in paragraph 5, will be governed for a day landing mainly by :—

(i) Suitability for landing and employing tanks.

(ii) Practicability of support by naval gunfire.

(iii) Suitability of the country for the establishment of a covering position.

72. These factors must be considered in conjunction with the facilities for defence which the physical characteristics of the landing places and neighbourhood may offer to the enemy.

73. To enable tanks to be employed, it will usually be necessary to land on a foreshore of flat rock, sand, firm shingle, or hard mud.

74. Within the limits of the locality selected for each distinct landing operation it will usually be advisable to land on as wide a front as practicable. The landing places on this front may be equally spaced or may be in groups, depending on the nature of the coastline. In either case the landing places should be divided up on a tactical basis, each main division or group being termed a "beach."

Huge volumes of supplies are taken ashore at Omaha beach, about a week after the initial landings.

75. When deciding on the locality or localities for the operation, consideration must be given to the employment of *Feints and Diversions*, and the localities in which they can be most profitably carried out.

76. *The state of the tide* must be considered. Most foreshores are steeper-to at high-water than at low, and mud foreshores are usually firmer. And at high-water there will be a shorter distance to advance before cover can be reached. The advantages of a rising tide in helping to refloat landing craft should be considered, but with power-driven craft this will be of comparatively minor importance.

77. *Currents and tidal streams* along the beach must also be considered. For landing tanks it may be essential for the landing craft to be at right angles to the beach. Where there are strong tidal streams this may only be possible at the turn of the stream—which will not usually be at the same time as the turn of the tide.

Support by Ships and Aircraft[1]

78. To enable the landing to be achieved despite enemy opposition, support by ships and aircraft may be required in any or all of the following forms:—

  (i) *High-explosive bombardment* from ships or aircraft and *machine-gun attack* from aircraft—to neutralize enemy fire and to delay reinforcements.

[. . .] Landing the First Flight

118. On arrival of ships carrying the assaulting force in the position at which the troops are to be transferred to the landing craft, all first flight landing craft not already in the water must be hoisted out or lowered, and such as are not carried in, or in tow of, the ships carrying the forces destined for them must proceed alongside the ships to which they are detailed. The arrangements necessary to ensure this will include a "Landing Craft Table"

---

1 Certain nations have been carrying out experiments in landing a force of troops from aircraft by means of parachutes. Such a force would probably suffer certain important disadvantages, *e.g.*, the descent of any considerable number of men by parachute would be extremely conspicuous, and their subsequent freedom of movement would be limited by lack of transport and difficulties of maintenance. It would also be difficult to prevent the landing being spread over a considerable area and this would necessitate its being made at some distance from enemy troops so as to allow the force to concentrate before being called on to fight. At the time of publication of this book, Therefore, the tactical value of such a force appears small. Technical developments, however, may overcome some of the main difficulties and, in this event, the value of landing such a force a short distance inland in order to attack beach defences in reverse might be considerable.

drawn up by the naval and military authorities in collaboration when any part of the force is landing from transports, the P.S.TO

119. When the force is being landed from transports, important points will be —

(i) If ships with specially fitted holds for the carriage of fuelled tanks and other vehicles cannot be made available, the petrol required will be stowed in cans on the decks of ships carrying the tanks and fuelling will be carried out on deck. All possible arrangements should be made to minimize the delay in disembarkation which this method may entail. If, for instance, weather and other conditions permit, a proportion of the tanks allotted to the "first flight" might be stowed on deck already fuelled.

(ii) Arrangements for hoisting out M.L.Cs, and loading them with tanks (either before or after hoisting out).

120. When the force is being landed from warships, it is probable that all tanks included in the first flight will already be in landing craft and that these will be in tow of the ships carrying the tanks' crews.

121. Arrangements for the conduct of the operation subsequent to the landing craft proceeding alongside ships carrying troops must include details for—

(i) *Transfer of troop* from ships to landing craft, including method of assembly in the ship, ladders, to be used by each unit, and allocation of troops to landing craft.

(ii) *Organization of landing craft* in groups as required for the various landing places, and their assembly in accordance with this organization.

(iii) *Timing.*—It will usually be desirable to arrange that all first flight troops arrive at all beaches simultaneously. To ensure this, the times at which the landing craft leave the places of assembly must be accurately calculated. Zero hour will as a rule be the time at which the first group or groups of landing craft go ahead. It will not usually be possible to decide on the exact clock time of zero hour before this event and it must therefore be signalled at the time.

122. The method of signalling zero hour will require careful consideration to ensure that it is received by all concerned and to prevent it jeopardising surprise. For a large force landing at dawn it may be difficult to reconcile these two requirements.

123. The timing of all movements prior to the landing craft going ahead must be based on an estimated zero hour.

124. The control of landing craft while on passage to the shore and the conduct of the troops embarked in them will be governed by the same instructions as for a night landing.

125. Should landing craft be attacked with *Gas* sprayed by aircraft, any parts contaminated should at once be scrubbed with salt water, and long handled scrubbers must be carried for this purpose. When there is any probability of such attacks, both the troops and the crews should be provided with light anti-gas clothing. In the event of serious contamination of landing craft, particularly wooden boats, they must return for decontamination after landing their troops. Previous arrangements must be made for ships to carry out this duty if required.

126. The possibility of *Underwater Obstructions* (*see* Appendix XV) off the landing places must be considered, and they must be avoided or dealt with as circumstances permit. M.L.Cs, and motor lighters will probably be able to penetrate hastily constructed obstructions without much difficulty.

127. The existence of previously undiscovered natural off-shore obstructions, either rocks or shoals, must also be considered. Everything possible must be done, by sounding and a sharp look-out, to avoid such obstructions and land at the most suitable place.

128. Should unexpectedly severe opposition or underwater obstructions, either natural or artificial, make it impossible to land in the vicinity intended, the naval officer in charge of the group of landing craft (or senior officer of the several groups in that vicinity), in conjunction with the military officer accompanying him and guided by any previous instructions he may have received, will decide the position to which the landing craft are to be diverted.

129. As already indicated, a daylight landing against opposition will normally be covered by naval bombardment and screened by smoke. Despite this, however, avoidance of delay by the landing craft in beaching themselves in the best way for efficient disembarkation and the mobility and dash of the leading troops will be matters of great importance. The landing of the first flight should whenever possible be direct from landing craft without the employment of any devices other than the ramps with which they may be equipped. In exceptional circumstances rafts, towed by the landing craft and pushed into place ahead of them when they ground, might be used to decrease the depth of water into which the infantry would otherwise have to disembark and the distance they would have to wade. In most cases, however, the difficulty of placing such rafts and their exposure to fire would outweigh the advantages. Should such devices be required they would be provided by the navy.

130. Also of importance will be the relative times and positions at which landing craft for a particular beach reach the shore. It will usually be advisable

to effect the landing at each beach over as wide a front as practicable, so as to force the enemy to disperse his fire. A simultaneous and rapidly completed landing at all points will also be advisable as a rule; but where the landing is to take place against a considerable number of unneutralized machine guns the first troops to land must be tanks and the disembarkation of infantry may have to be delayed until the action of the tanks has begun to neutralize the hostile machine guns.

131. In addition to the troops required for capturing the beaches the first flight will include certain personnel (Signals, N.F.O.Os. and Artillery) who will be required ashore as soon as the beaches have been cleared of the enemy. It must be arranged as far as possible that these officers and men do not become involved in the fighting for the beaches, and it may even be advisable to transport them in a separate landing craft which will not reach the shore until after the beaches are captured.

132. The task of the first flight is to secure the beach and its immediate surroundings so as to enable the rest of the assaulting force to land under its protection. It must be given a definite objective which will include any position from which aimed small arms fire can be brought to bear on the beach. It must also be given the definite task of dealing with any known hostile machine guns in the vicinity of the beach.

133. The greatest determination must be shown by the first flight in its capture of the beaches, since it is on the success of this that the success of the whole operation depends. Troops must press on at all costs and must be prepared to make up for any deficiencies in covering fire by the use of their own close support weapons. It is of importance that early information of the progress of the first flight should reach the O.C. Assaulting Force afloat.

134. When most of the landing craft are employed with the first flight (as will usually be the case), there will be a considerable interval, depending mainly on the distance of the ships from the beaches, before the next flight is landed. The first flight troops must, therefore, be so equipped as to maintain themselves during this period.

[…]

Landing the Second and Subsequent Flights

142. Subject to any special orders to meet changes in the tactical situation (which would be given by the S.N.O.L. at the instance of the O.C. Assaulting Force), the disembarkation of the second and subsequent flights should be carried out in accordance with a pre-arranged programme drawn up by the naval and military authorities and the P.S.T.O. in collaboration.

143. To enable the disembarkation to be carried out efficiently the beaches must be organized and piers and beach-roadways constructed, as indicated in

the next chapter, organization and construction proceeding concurrently with the landing. Whether the beach parties should land in the first flight landing craft or subsequently will depend on circumstances. They must not become involved in the fighting for the beach but will be required ashore as soon as the immediate vicinity of the beach has been cleared of the enemy.

144. As soon as the first flight troops have landed, the landing craft must return as quickly as possible to the ships to which they are assigned in the programme of disembarkation.

145. Arrangements must be made for the disposal of men who have been wounded or killed in the landing craft—either to the shore or to hospital ships. Under no circumstances should wounded men be taken back to ships which are still landing troops.

146. Some casualties to and disorganization of landing craft of the first flight must be expected. The troops landing in subsequent flights should therefore not be detailed for individual craft, but should be drawn up in the order in which they are to land and detailed as the craft return. Whether, after loading, the landing craft proceed ashore independently or in groups will depend on the tactical situation.

147. Similar arrangements must be made for the landing of tanks, guns and M.T. vehicles. These arrangements will require careful collaboration between the military authorities and the P.S.T.O. to ensure marrying vehicles and their crews if in separate ships.

148. A naval officer should be detailed by the S.N.O.L. to exercise a general control of the landing craft and to ensure as far as possible that the programme of disembarkation is adhered to. He must work in close co-operation with the military authorities, the P.S.T.O. and the Principal Beach Master and endeavour to meet their requirements in landing craft throughout the operations. He will be responsible for any re-allocation of landing craft that may necessary owing to casualties or to a change in the disembarkation programme. He will also be responsible in conjunction with the commanding officers of the depôt ships off the beaches for the repair of damaged landing craft and for the arrangements of periodical reliefs of their crews. He should be provided with a separate power boat for his own exclusive use.

149. As soon as the assaulting force has gained a sufficient footing ashore to cover the approaches to the beaches from machine-gun fire, the landing craft previously employed can be reinforced by horse boats, dumb lighters, transports' lifeboats and naval cutters, towed by steamboats and motorboats. When cutters and lifeboats are used prior to the construction of piers or landing stages, it will be an advantage if the boats are fitted with gang-planks to allow the troops to land dry shod.

Operations of the Assaulting Force after Landing

150. The task of the assaulting force as a whole is to secure the beaches and shipping from ground-observed artillery fire. A definite objective must be given and there must be no delay in pushing forward to reach it. It is essential to make ground as quickly as possible while the enemy is still disorganized by the surprise of the landing and before he can get reinforcements. If the objective is not gained during this period it may never be reached.

151. The advance must be part of a definite plan and must be properly organized. The plan must, however, be flexible, since not only may it not be known beforehand what the scale of enemy resistance will be, but also it will not be known for certain at which beaches it will be possible to effect a landing.

152. The organization of the command of the assaulting force must, therefore, be such as to ensure that there is no lack of coordinated effort between the forces landed at different beaches. In order to ensure this it will generally be necessary for the O.C., Assaulting Force, to delegate a considerable

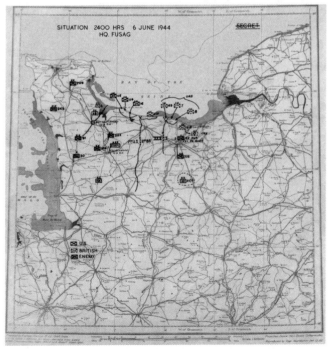

A FUSAG situation map showing the tactical situation at midnight on 6 June 1944.

amount of authority to his subordinates, more particularly during the period prior to the time at which he himself lands.

Floating Reserve

153. The organization of a part of the assaulting force as a Floating Reserve will usually be advisable, so as to permit success to be exploited to the greatest possible extent. This will be particularly the case when simultaneous landings are being effected over a considerable stretch of coast line. By exploiting those landings which are most successful, positions from which all can be covered may be more quickly attained than by endeavouring to achieve a uniform advance from each beach.

CHAPTER 5

CONSOLIDATION

For Rommel and Rundstedt in the hours following the Allied landings in Normandy, there was a rapidly closing window of opportunity. This has been described as the 'battle of the build-up', the period in which the Allies tried to consolidate their grip on the occupied shore through both offensive movement forward and the rapid influx of additional logistics and men. This enterprise was essentially the effort to turn a fragile foothold into a permanent and secure base of operations.

It was a battle that the Allies won. Now that the gate was open, the Allied build-up rushed in. By the end of June 1944, more than 850,000 men, nearly 150,000 vehicles and 570,500 tons of supplies had been shipped into France, a force that would keep growing and would eventually take back France, Belgium and drive into Germany itself. But before wider Europe could be claimed back from the Germans, the Allies had to secure their gains and then push out into the interior of Normandy and face a Wehrmacht fighting tenaciously to stem off defeat.

This chapter brings together a range of resources that speak not only of the consolidation of the beachheads, but also the tactical considerations of fighting in the complex rural landscape of Normandy, which with its narrow lanes, thick hedgerows and dense woodland favoured the defence. D-Day had given the Allies access to Europe, but for many weeks victory seemed a very distant prospect indeed.

Landing Operations on Hostile Shores (1941)

CHAPTER 5
OPERATIONS ON SHORE
Section III Beachhead

133. **Beachhead.**—The first consideration in the conduct of operations on shore after the landing has been effected is the seizure of a beachhead of sufficient extent to insure the continuous landing of troops and matériel, and to secure the terrain features and maneuver space requisite for the

projected operations on shore. The establishment of a beachhead enables a commander to maintain control of his forces until the situation ashore has developed and he has sufficient information on which to base his plans and orders for further operations. As a matter of security, it is necessary to clear the beachhead of enemy resistance. It should be kept in mind, however, that the establishment of a beachhead is not a purely defensive measure. It has the equally important object of insuring further advance inland if required to accomplish the mission of the force. Consideration is given therefore to the early seizure of terrain features which will facilitate this advance by

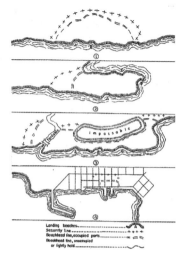

Figure 15.

including them in the beachhead or making them the objective of a special operation. Consideration is also given to depriving the enemy of terrain features which are most advantageous to him in the defense.

134. **Beachhead Line.**—The beachhead line is an objective prescribed for the purpose of fixing the limits of the beachhead. It is not necessarily a defensive position to be occupied and organized as such. It is, however, a tentative main line of resistance in case of counterattack prior to the advance from the beachhead, and it is occupied and organized to the extent demanded by the situation (see fig. 15).

135. **Reconnaissance and Security Line.**—

    a. The security line is one which prescribes the minimum distance beyond the beachhead line to which security detachments will be pushed by units occupying the beachhead line. Active reconnaissance will be conducted in the prescribed zone by designated units. The designation of the line prevents a greater dispersion of the force as a whole than is described by the beachhead force commander (see fig. 15).

    b. The reconnaissance and security line for landing operations differs from that employed in other ground operations in that it is normally closer to the beachhead line (the tentative main line of resistance) and becomes the outpost line in case the beachhead line is occupied for defense, whereas in other ground operations the reconnaissance and security line is normally in advance of the outpost line. it must be far enough in advance to protect the beachhead line from surprise ground attack and screen it from hostile ground observation and attack.

136. **Extent and Form of Beachhead.—**

    a. The beachhead should be of sufficient depth and frontage to protect the landing points from medium artillery fire. Usually, this will be possible only with comparatively large forces. A landing force must guard against over extension of its units with consequent endangering of its flanks, beach establishments, and land lines of communications. The depth and frontage of the beachhead will be dependent upon the mission, the size of the force engaged, the nature of the terrain particularly as regards natural obstacles, and the probable enemy reaction.

    b. Figure 15 shows diagrammatically how terrain features may modify the form of the beachhead, and the extent to which the beachhead line may have to be occupied under various conditions in order to insure the desired security of the shore establishments. In figure 15(1), the terrain is assumed to be suitable for maneuver throughout its whole extent. In figure 15(2) and (3), the effect is shown of certain impassable obstacles which may be encountered in a variety of forms and combinations. Figure 15(4) shows a beachhead where it is necessary to land in a town. In most situations of this kind it would be advisable to land outside the town unless only very weak resistance is anticipated or complete surprise is practicable.

137. **Successive Objectives.**—The commander of the landing force may designate successive objectives to coordinate the advance from the beach to the beachhead line. these successive objectives have the advantage of permitting reorganization of attacking troops, passage of lines, coordination of field artillery and ships' gunfire with the advance, and of facilitating the execution of an appreciable change in direction of the attack. Successive objectives may entail delay and should not be prescribed unless actually needed for a definite purpose.

138. **Intermediate Beachhead Lines.—**

    a. Subordinate commanders may find it desirable to prescribe intermediate objectives or beachhead lines for their units, particularly when the landing force commander has not prescribed successive objectives. If successive objectives have been designated, these usually serve the purpose of intermediate beachhead lines, at least for major subdivisions of the landing force. Lower echelons, particularly when beaches are not contiguous, may require intermediate beachhead lines short of the first of the successive objectives prescribed by the superior commanders in order to reorganize, bring forward supporting weapons, or to establish liaison with adjacent combat teams. When intermediate beachhead lines are prescribed, they are designated CT (combat team)—1st Objective,—Infantry, 1st Objective, and son on, according to the unit for which prescribed.

b. Prescribing intermediate beachhead lines is desirable because disorganization and loss of control may result during the ship-to-shore movement and the initial advance ashore, particularly when strong opposition is encountered. The establishment of an intermediate beachhead enables the commander to regain control of his unit and to maintain control of it until he has sufficient information on which to base his plans and orders for further advance. It also provides security for the landing of the rear elements of the unit. The prescribing of intermediate beachhead lines must not be allowed to cause unnecessary delay in the advance. On arrival at these lines, no halt should be made if the situation is such that the advance can be continued.

c. The intermediate beachhead line prescribed by the commander of a major subordinate element of a landing force as large as a division should, if practicable, protect the landing beaches of the unit against hostile light artillery fire. A regimental or battalion (combat team) beachhead line should protect the landing beaches of the regiment against effective small-arms fire.

139. **Establishing Beachhead.**—In a landing operation, troops must clear the beach rapidly. There must be no delay at the water's edge. This requires that leading units be landed in assault formation as fully deployed as the available boats permit. Once landed, every individual must thoroughly understand that he must clear the beach promptly and move rapidly inland or in the designated direction. Assault units push the attack to their designated objectives without waiting for the advance of units on their flanks. If a unit is landed on a beach other than that designated for its landing, its commander will initiate such action as will best further the general scheme of maneuver.

140. **Advance From Beachhead.**—The desirability of establishing a security zone around his shore base should not lead a landing force commander to adopt a defensive attitude after the beachhead is secured. Any mission other than merely holding the beachhead is best accomplished by aggressive action, and aggressive action often affords the best protection to the beach establishments. The advance from the beachhead line however may entail the breaking of contact with the shore on one or both flanks and the establishment

of shore lines of communication. Under such conditions, the securing of a beachhead may be followed by a period of stabilization for the necessary regrouping of forces. Reconnaissances by aviation and ground troops should be pushed vigorously during reorganization and the delay on the beachhead line reduced to the minimum. During this phase, liaison between naval aviation and ground troops may be difficult but is highly important.

Section IV
Scheme of Maneuver

141. **General.**—The decision as to the scheme of maneuver to be adopted by the landing force is affected by many allied decisions which are discussed in other sections of this manual. Some of these decisions are—

    a. Determination of the landing area to be utilized, which is dependent on the expected opposition, the character of available beaches, suitability of the terrain for shore operations, configuration of the coast line, the effect of the time element in reaching objectives, and similar factors.

    b. Selection of the time of landing, which is based on the relative advantages and disadvantages of daylight and darkness for the specific operation in prospect.

    c. Decision as to the formation to be adopted for the ship-to-shore movement, which is determined by a consideration of the strength and composition of the landing force, available boats, size of beaches, prospective action after landing, and similar conditions.

    d. The naval gunfire and aviation support to be furnished (see chs. 6 and 7).

142. **Frontage of Attack.**—

    a. The frontage to be covered by the landings and the subsequent advance inland is an important consideration in formulating the scheme of maneuver. The frontage of the landing is dependent to a large extent upon the number, type, and relative position of the beaches available in the landing area. The strength and equipment of the attacking force, is, however, an almost equally important consideration. During the initial stages of the landing, ship's guns and aviation provide the artillery in support of the attacking force. the attacking force therefore comprises two elements of major importance, namely the landing force and naval and aviation support.

    b. The landing force attacks on a wide front in order to increase the speed of landing and to cause a dispersion of the defender's efforts, but it must not overextend. It must concentrate its effort and assign sufficient forces to the various tasks to insure their success. Units comprising initial assault echelons are particularly apt to become disorganized during and immediately after the landing, and they cannot be expected to make deep penetrations against strong opposition. Therefore, leading assault units usually secure an intermediate beachhead and cover the landing of additional troops. In many cases landings are not made on the entire front of the beachhead. This results in the zone of attack increasing in width as the advance progresses. The scheme of maneuver therefore must provide for the introduction of additional units in the assault from time to time in order to take care of this increased front. Sufficient reserves must be kept in hand to insure the exploitation of successes and to continue the attack to the final objective. The success of the initial effort is of first consideration and the forces necessary to its success must be assigned before thought can be given to reserves for future contingencies. An operation which initially requires all of the attacker's forces to secure the foothold on the beach is rarely justified. Units must be assigned frontages which permit a depth of formation commensurate with the effort expected of them.

[. . .]

c. Naval gunfire and combat aviation must be concentrated in support of the landing. Even a relatively small number of enemy machine guns and light artillery pieces firing under favorable conditions have a devastating effect on units as they approach and land on the beach. Assault units will probably be unable to get ashore and advance against this fire unless adequately supported by ship fire and combat aviation. A landing attack must not be held up while naval support groups are moved in order to augment inadequate supporting fires arranged for initially. Usually there is only one opportunity for a successful landing. Successive efforts subsequent to an attack which has failed are increasingly difficult. It is necessary therefore to limit the landings to frontages which are commensurate with the amount of supporting fire available. The scheme of maneuver may provide for adequate fire support either by restricting the landing to beaches of such number and extent as can be supported by all available ships and aviation, or by landings echeloned in time so that ships and available aviation can support the landings in turn.

143. **Influence of Landing Boats.**—The speed with which troops can be put ashore depends upon the number and type of boats available and the distance of the transports from the various beaches. The scheme of maneuver

therefore must take these factors into consideration, particularly where there are not enough boats to embark all of the landing force at one time. The timely support of assault echelons and the prompt exploitation of success require reserves in boats immediately available. This limits the number of boats and consequently the troops and frontages which can be assigned the initial assault echelons. The frontage of the initial attack is affected also by the number of small fast boats available for assault troops. Such boats should be provided for the leading platoons of battalions which are to be landed in assault. All boats in any group should have the same speed. Slower boats should be used where speed is not of vital importance.

144. **Hostile Disposition.**—Beaches strongly organized for defense are avoided, if possible, in the initial landings. Advantage is taken of undefended or lightly defended portions of the shore line, even though they present less favorable landing conditions, in order to outmaneuver the hostile resistance or to gain a position from which flanking artillery or small-arms fire may assist the landing at more favorable beaches.

145. **Landing by Echelon.**—If a simultaneous landing cannot be made on all selected landing beaches, the landing may be made by echelon. In attacking by echelon it is generally desirable to land the last echelon at the beach, or beaches, where it is planned to make the main effort. this enables the ships which support that landing to continue without interruption in support of the advance of the main effort. Plans must be flexible, however, and constant consideration is given to the advisability of exploiting a landing already successfully executed rather than attempting a new landing against opposition. The time interval between landings in an attack by echelon may vary between wide limits. Where there are sufficient boats to carry all of the landing force in one trip and the supporting ships can cover the various landings from the same general locality, this interval may be only a few minutes. The amount of ship gunfire to be placed on the various beaches, together with the scheme of maneuver on shore, will determine this time interval. Where two or more boat trips and considerable movement of the supporting ships are required, or where it is desired to cause a movement of hostile reserves toward the first landing, several hours may elapse between landings. The danger of being defeated in detail must be guarded against. Landings by echelon should be attempted only when the beaches, or groups of beaches, are separated by sufficient distances that troops landed on one beach will not be endangered by naval gunfire on another beach. A landing by echelon, as in a landing on a single beach, facilitates the concentration of the hostile artillery fires. In connection with such landings, demonstrations should be made to cause a dispersion of the hostile fire. In addition, heavy counterbattery fire or combat aviation should be employed to neutralize the enemy batteries.

'How British deal with road craters, obstacles' was an article published in the US Military Intelligence Service's *Intelligence Bulletin* in August 1943. It has a special resonance for D-Day, as without the epic efforts of Allied engineers it would have been almost impossible to get the landing forces off the beaches and onwards into France. Engineer units were intermingled with every assault force, and were tasked with duties ranging from demolishing beach obstacles through to laying solid surfaces on which armour and other vehicles could advance. Following the massive amount of bombing and shelling of the Normandy coastline, furthermore, many troops – engineers and infantry alike – would have been committed to repairing roads holed by craters and barred by obstacles, and this document illustrates some of the British approaches to these problems.

'How British deal with road craters, obstacles' (1943)

1. INTRODUCTION

In the British Army, troops of all arms are instructed how to deal with road craters and road obstacles when prompt action is required in an emergency. The following is an extract from a British Army document on this subject:

2. CRATERS

First, look for antitank mines, antipersonnel mines, and booby traps, within or around the craters. Then look for a detour and use it if possible, cutting down fences and ramping all low banks. If a suitable detour exists, it will nearly always be more advisable to use it than to repair the crater.

If it is necessary to fill in the craters, slightly different methods will be used for dry and wet craters.

a. Dry Craters

Trample down all loose earth inside the crater.
Start filling the crater with all the loose soil available. As soon as the depth has been sufficiently reduced, a tracked vehicle should be driven across the crater to consolidate the soil, and this procedure repeated at intervals. Where brushwood is available, alternate layers of brushwood and soil should be laid. The brushwood will help to consolidate the soil, and at the same time distribute the load. Any rock, stone, or gravel thrown up by the explosion should be saved, and used later in making the road surface.

Continue filling until the depth of the crater has been reduced to 3 feet. As a rule, any filled-in craters of this depth will be passable for tracked vehicles, ¾-ton trucks, and even 1½-ton trucks.

If it is essential to make a passage for all military vehicles, cut ramps on opposite sides of the crater, and shovel the soil from these two cuts into the crater. If each ramp is cut 10 feet long, enough soil will be made available to reduce the depth of the average crater so that it will be passable for all vehicles.

The surfacing of a filled-in crater should be completed before any but the most essential vehicles are permitted to cross, unless the crater is completely dry and likely to remain so. Otherwise, vehicles crossing over will churn up the soil and soon render further crossing impossible. The surfacing should consist of the stones and gravel which have been reserved for this purpose or of fascines [brushwood bundles]. A maintenance party will be needed to look after the surface until an engineer repair party can take over.

The following table may be used as a guide to indicate the time and labor required for crater filling. If a party of 20 men, equipped with picks, shovels, and axes, go to work on a dry crater 25 feet in diameter and 7 feet deep, in medium soil, they can make it passable for

tracked vehicles _ _ _ _ _ _ _ _ _ _ in 30 minutes

"4 × 4" (all-wheel-drive) trucks _ _ _ _ _ _ _ _ _ _ _ in 35 minutes

¾-ton trucks _ _ _ _ _ _ _ _ _ _ _ in 40 minutes

all vehicles except buses _ _ _ _ _ _ _ _ _ _ _ in 75 minutes

all vehicles _ _ _ _ _ _ _ _ _ _ _ in three hours

b. Wet Craters

If a crater contains water, a modification of the above procedure will be necessary.

If rocks and stones are available, use them to fill the crater up to water level. If there are no rocks or stones at hand, fill the crater bottom with earth. Cover this with two layers of empty sandbags to form a seal. Lay 9 inches of brushwood, and then 9 inches of earth. Repeat this sequence of empty sandbags, brushwood, and earth until the depth of the crater has been reduced to 3 feet. Layers should be laid so that they slope upward toward the center of the road to allow for consolidation of the center.

After this, follow the procedure outlined for filling a dry crater.

Water-filled craters naturally take slightly longer to improve than dry craters.

3. OTHER ROAD OBSTACLES

Hastily contrived road obstacles—such as farm wagons, the wheels of which have been removed, or felled trees—will often be fairly easy to destroy or move. However, it should be taken for granted that they will be liberally bobby-trapped. There will seldom be enough time to wait for skilled engineer personnel to locate and neutralize these traps. Therefore, the first troops to arrive on the site will find it necessary to set off the traps by using hand grenades or by tying ropes to the obstacle and, from a safe distance, hauling it off the road. It must also be remembered that antitank mines will probably have been laid in the road underneath the obstacle for this reason, an extremely careful examination of the road surface is a necessity.

Finally, it is strongly emphasized that if any possible detour exists, it is normally much quicker to go around an obstacle than to remove it. It must be expected that detours or obvious turnouts will be imaginatively mined and booby-trapped.

Another *Intelligence Bulletin* article, 'How the Germans Fight in Wooded and Broken Terrain' was actually published after the campaign in Normandy, but brought together the experiences of that campaign. The Allies were frequently frustrated at the slow progress they made in Normandy. Every lane, copse, tree line, farm, hill, village and town seemed to be contested, and the Germans showed real skill and tenacity in launching repeated ambushes and in constructing highly defendable positions with interlocking fields of fire. Often it was only the Allied fire superiority, accented by ground-attack sorties from the air, that broke a German defence.

'How the Germans Fight in Wooded and Broken Terrain' (1945)

The Germans recognize that operations in wooded and broken terrain require special combat methods both in the attack and in the defense. In such terrain the Germans try to control all roads and trails, so as to ensure the movement of support weapons and supplies. The heaviest fighting therefore generally takes place in the vicinity of these roads and trails.

GENERAL PRINCIPLES

In the attack the Germans maintain careful protective fire as they advance along the roads and trails; when they are obliged to move across open stretches, this protective fire becomes continuous. Roads are opened up as rapidly as possible, and are covered with antitank guns. Special attention is paid to the formations adopted during movement and in battle, to correct employment of fire power, to appropriate communication methods, to the problem of maintaining direction, and to supplying forward elements with an adequate amount of ammunition.

In the defense it is considered essential to block roads and trails. Snipers are posted in trees. Centers of resistance are established at curves, bends, and defiles, and whenever a road climbs to higher ground. Firing positions are prepared just off roads and trails, to command open fields of fire.

"In the defense it is considered essential to block roads and trails. Snipers are posted in trees. Centers of resistance are established at curves and defiles, and whenever a road climbs to higher ground."

METHOD OF ADVANCE

In the approach march, squads and platoons advance on a narrow front, deployed in depth along roadside hedges and scrub growth, and in hollows running in the desired direction. The leading squads, on contact, serve as scouts and patrols. They advance in extended order, with a light machine gun leading. While the squads immediately behind the forward squads deploy less deeply at intervals of 30 to 40 paces, the subsequent squads follow in squad columns so as to have all-around observation and protection. Special observers are detailed to watch out for tree snipers.

"In the approach march, squads and platoons advance on a narrow front, deployed in depth along roadside hedges and scrub growth."

The Germans believe that when battle is joined, the same formations employed during the approach march should be maintained as far as possible. Fire cover is provided by the support weapons, especially the mortars, which advance with the forward troops. However, the Germans recognize that further deployment of squads and platoons may be necessary. It is a German principle that after resistance has been crushed and hostile strong points eliminated, the original formations should be resumed immediately.

The reserve platoon advances, employing the same close formation, in the rear of the platoon which gains the most ground. The commander of the reserve platoon arranges for all-around protection, particularly to repel surprise attacks which may be made by hostile forces from centers of resistance not yet engaged. These protective measures also include protection of the rear.

USE OF FIRE POWER

To eliminate centers of resistance, the Germans employ all available light and heavy weapons, especially mortars.

Since observation in close country is difficult, the Germans not only keep their support weapons well forward, but often use their heavy machine guns as light machine guns.

Terrain conditions are likely to have a definite effect on German employment of mortars. Sometimes observers can work only from treetops. Every effort is made to place observers close to the mortar positions so that

"Sometimes observers can work only from treetops."

"In the heat of battle, disk signaling is preferred."

"The antitank guns take over the job of preventing hostile tanks from using the roads."

corrections can be passed accurately and rapidly to the mortar detachment. The employment of message runners is not considered practicable in the heat of battle; instead, disk signaling is preferred. The Germans try not to site their mortars too close to the roadside scrub growth.

The commanders of the support weapons are required to report their availability to the leading rifle company commander and his platoon commanders, and to remain in their vicinity.

The antitank guns follow without orders in the rear of the infantry, as soon as the roads have been cleared. Their principal mission is to take over the job of preventing hostile tanks from using the roads. In addition, so far as their principal mission permits, the antitank guns take part in attacks on Allied centers of resistance, using antitank high-explosive shells.

Protected by the fire of the support weapons, the infantry works its way forward as close as possible to the Allied centers of resistance. As soon as the support weapons cease firing, the infantry breaks through, hurling hand grenades. The Germans are scrupulously careful in regulating the time when the support weapons are to cease firing—first the medium mortars and then the heavy machine guns—and the time when the breakthrough is to be attempted. The points at which the breakthrough is to be made are sealed off on the flanks by squads especially detailed for this job. Hostile positions along hedges or other roadside growth are mopped-up after the breakthrough.

MISCELLANEOUS PRECAUTIONS

Platoons and squads detail men for the express purpose of maintaining contact with neighboring units. These men indicate the headquarters of their own units by means of pennants and by signaling with lamps to flanking squads and platoons. It is a rule that pennants marked "Front Line" always be put up. Identification panels are laid out, when necessary, to indicate the advance of the front line.

Because the opportunities for unobserved movement are very good in terrain of this type, the Germans make considerable use of runners. Radio-telegraphy and smoke cartridges also are used, in addition to the light signals.

"Compass directions are issued before the departure."

"Because of terrain difficulties, the Germans find it useful to equip squads with ladders, axes, good knives, and sharp spades."

Higher headquarters are continually kept informed about the situation, to permit smooth coordination of the attack.

Since the problem of maintaining direction is difficult in closely wooded and unevenly wooded terrain, squad leaders are given specific rendezvous on roads and paths. Compass directions are issued before the departure.

Because of terrain difficulties, the Germans find it useful to equip squads with ladders, axes, good knives, and sharp spades. Since ammunition supply is likely to be slow and cannot be relied upon, a generous quantity of ammunition, including hand grenades, is issued to the men before the departure.

In this final extract from the *Manual of Combined Operations*, the authors weighed the important considerations of what happened after a landing force had been placed ashore. For the Allied forces on the Normandy coastline in June 1944, the twin priorities were to build up the logistical infrastructure of the invasion and to fend off German counter-attacks. The latter were certainly coming in, and fighting intensified around the beachheads, but Hitler's belief that the real invasion would eventually come at the Pas-de-Calais meant that some valuable armoured reserves were held back when they could have been committed to the fight. Note that in terms of logistics, to overcome the lack of a proximate supply harbour (Cherbourg would not be captured fully until 1 July), the Allies transported across with them the components for two huge artificial harbours, known as 'MULBERRIES', which would provide docking and offloading facilities for the invasion fleet. The harbours alone were a magisterial achievement, together weighing more than 1.5 million tons and requiring the efforts of 10,000 men and 132 tugs to assemble, and they gave the Allies the initial facilities to achieve the logistical feats required to consolidate the invasion.

Manual of Combined Operations (1938)

CHAPTER 24
OPERATIONS SUBSEQUENT TO THE LANDING OF THE ASSAULTING FORCE

General Remarks

1. The course of events subsequent to the landing of the assaulting force will depend on the general nature of the operations as classified in Chapter 18, para. 1. It is convenient therefore to consider the various possibilities under different headings as follows :—

(i) Establishing a secure organization for the supply and reinforcement of the forces already landed.

(ii) Landing military forces and/or air forces for further offensive operations.

(iii) Supplying and reinforcing the forces already landed, without installing air defences at the point of landing.

(iv) Re-embarkation.

2. These activities, however, are not necessarily distinct and they may also overlap the landing of the assaulting force to some extent. Thus, the work to secure the maintenance of forces already landed may commence before the assaulting force has reached its covering position, and the landing of further forces may be concurrent with establishing a secure supply organization;

while, in the case of a raid, steps to facilitate re-embarkation may have to be taken shortly after the assaulting force has made good the landing.

3. A further combined operation which may be undertaken subsequently to a landing on a hostile shore, viz., the establishment of a fleet air or army base, is considered in Part VIII of this manual.

Section I.—SUPPLY AND REINFORCEMENT OF FORCES ALREADY LANDED

General Remarks

4. Assuming that the assaulting forces have established themselves in positions that cover the landing places from undue interference by enemy military forces, the problem of ensuring that their supply and reinforcement can be carried out continuously on any required scale resolves itself into :—

(i) Defence against surface vessels and submarines.

(ii) Defence against aircraft.

(iii) Organization and control of the unloading of the transports and the landing of supplies and reinforcements.

[. . .]

Defence against Surface Vessels and Submarines

5. The protection of the expedition against attack by powerful surface forces will be secured in the same manner as during the voyage, approach and landing of the assaulting force, i.e., by the operations of our naval forces either in the vicinity or in covering positions. The main requirements for protecting the expedition from naval interference subsequent to the landing of the assaulting force are therefore that the anchorages used for disembarkation should be protected against submarine attack and against night attack by small craft. In a prolonged operation involving shipping movements to and from sea, protection against minelaying will also be required.

6. Anti-submarine defence during this period, as during the landing of the assaulting force, will depend mainly on destroyer and small craft patrols assisted by aircraft. For prolonged operations these patrols may be assisted and to some extent replaced by :—

(i) Indicator nets.

(ii) Indicator loops.

(iii) Controlled minefields.

(iv) Anti-submarine booms.

(v) Anti-torpedo baffles.

7. The effectiveness of both mobile and fixed anti-submarine defences will depend in large measure on hydrographic conditions. As already stated in regard to landing the assaulting force, these conditions must be taken into account when selecting an anchorage for that operation. Further consideration must be given to them from the point of view of fixed defences when security of anchorages for supply and reinforcement over a prolonged period is concerned.

8. Defence against night attack will also consist mainly of patrols. As with anti-submarine defences, the effectiveness of the defence will be largely dependent on hydrographic factors. Under some conditions additional protection against M.T.B. attack may be effected by laying anti-boat booms, by mounting close-defence guns and searchlights ashore, and by anchoring warships in such positions that, though themselves protected by land, they can use their guns and searchlights against attacking craft.

9. Defence against mines will depend partly on the preventive effect of patrols, partly on the daily searching of established channels by minesweepers, and partly on the use of protector-paravanes by warships and transports proceeding to and from sea.

Defence against Aircraft

10. The measures for local air defence of the anchorages and beaches during the landing of the assaulting force (viz. :—anti-aircraft gunfire from ships and fighter patrols) are necessarily dependent on an exceptional effort which can only be maintained for a limited period, and are comparatively ineffectual at night once the landing has been discovered. When the area of operations is within reach of enemy aircraft, therefore, and the assaulting force needs continuous supply and reinforcement, these initial measures must be augmented and eventually superseded by a more permanent system of anti-aircraft defence, i.e., by guns and searchlights mounted ashore. As soon as the shore anti-aircraft defences have been established, the officer commanding them will be primarily responsible for local defence against aircraft.

11. When available, the anti-aircraft guns and searchlights of warships will be of value in adding to the volume of fire and illumination, but as ships' searchlights are not fitted with sound locators they will not usually be switched on until aircraft have been illuminated by shore lights. The shore and ship anti-aircraft defences must be co-ordinated in accordance with the principles laid down in the Manual of Coast Defence.

12. The operations of the air forces of the expedition subsequent to the landing will contribute generally to the security of the position, but a proportion of the available bomber effort and the operations of the fighters may have to be co-ordinated with the anti-aircraft defensive arrangements. The extent to which this will be required will depend on the local air situation.

13. The main difficulties confronting the establishment of efficient air defences will be :—

    (i) To site the guns and particularly the lights in sufficient depth.

    (ii) To site the guns and lights so as to cover the anchorage.

    (iii) To institute an efficient warning system.

14. The possibilities of establishing a warning system to landward will depend on circumstances. To seaward and along the coast the use of ships and small craft for this purpose must be considered.

15. As already indicated, the assaulting force must be landed without the protection of shore anti-aircraft defences (except possibly light A.A. batteries), but these defences must be installed before landing supplies and reinforcements on a large scale. The detailed arrangements for landing guns and lights must depend on circumstances. It may be practicable to land some of them during the later stages of the landing of the assaulting force, and, provided sufficient landing craft are available, it will not usually be necessary to postpone the land to postpone the landing of supplies and reinforcements until all the anti-aircraft defences have been landed and established.

Organization and Control of Unloading the Transports and Landing Supplies and Reinforcements

16. The principal ways in which the landing of supplies and reinforcements will differ from the landing of the assaulting for are :—

    (i) The protection afforded to the beaches, by the establishment of the assaulting force in a covering position, may enable the work of landing supplies, stores, vehicles, etc., to be taken over by civilian personnel.

    (ii) Progress in the building of piers and construction of beach roadways will lead to the employment of fewer, but better equipped, landing points.

    (iii) For landing the assaulting force reliance may have beenplaced on a spell of favourable weather, but for continuous supply and reinforcement provision against bad weather must be made. This may entail using different anchorages and beaches from those employed for the landing of the assaulting force.

17. The general organization required for unloading the transports and the organization of the beaches will be on the same lines as during the landing of the assaulting force and will be arranged by the military and air force authorities (particularly the M.L.O. and R.A.F.L.O.), the S.N.O.L., the P.S.T.O. and the P.B.M. in collaboration. Should the control of the landing be taken over by the

Board of Trade, the S.N.O.L. would no longer play any part in the organization and the P.B.M. would be relieved by an officer of the Board of Trade.

18. The decision as to when the landing operations are sufficiently free from enemy interference to permit the work to be carried out as a matter of routine by civilian personnel will be made by the Naval Commander. When this situation arises, control of the landing of troops, animals, weapons, vehicles and supplies will be taken over by the P.S.T.O. as the representative of the Board of Trade. This control will extend to the "line of demarcation" on the beaches.

19. On the Board of Trade taking over responsibility for the landing, civilian personnel will be provided for beach parties and landing craft from commercial sources.

20. During this period the military and air force working parties on the beaches may be replaced by a military or air force labour corps or by civilian labour under military or air force direction.

21. The construction of piers and beach roadways, and also the general progress of the operations, will tend towards concentrating the landing at those landing places which are most suitable and most completely equipped. In addition to concentrating at some of those landing places already in use, the possibility of employing more suitable landing places elsewhere must also be considered.

22. Suitability of the landing places for furthering the military operations must be decided by the army, and it is also the army's responsibility to equip the landing places with the piers and roadways required. These factors must be considered in conjunction with naval responsibilities for the protection of shipping from naval action and for the safety of shipping and landing craft from the effect of the weather (see para. 25 below) before a decision is reached regarding the landing places to be employed for a prolonged operation. The safety of shipping against air attack, which is a combined naval, military and air force responsibility (see paras. 10–12 above). may also enter into the decision.

23. As already indicated (Chapter 23, para. 9), responsibility for designing and constructing piers and laying beach roadways rests with the army, but it may be necessary for the military authorities to call for naval assistance in providing and mooring floating pier-heads, and in providing, placing and sinking lighters or other vessels to form the foundations or core of a fixed pier.

24. Anchorages taken up by transports during the landing of supplies and reinforcements should be organized in accordance with the landing places to which they are discharging, i.e., so as to reduce distances between transports and landing places as much as possible, having due regard to safety

of navigation and protection from naval and air attack. Organization of the anchorages and of movements to and from them will be a naval responsibility.

25. To guard against interruption of the landing operations by bad weather it may be necessary to :—

(i) Construct breakwaters sheltering the landing places.

(ii) Move the anchorages and landing places from the positions used during the landing of the assaulting force to more sheltered positions.

26. The construction of breakwaters, if required and if practicable, will be undertaken by the navy. The quickest method of improvising a breakwater is to use old ships, lighters, etc., scuttling them in the required positions and, if possible, filling them with concrete.

27. The establishment of the assaulting force in a secure position, coupled with the more deliberate nature of subsequent operations, may enable anchorages and landing places to be used which are more sheltered than those used for the original landing. The position taken up by the assaulting force may, in fact, have to be considered with this end in view. The use of more sheltered anchorages will also, in all probability, simplify the problem of anti-submarine defence (see para. 7 above) and possibly the problem of air defence.

28. If the nature of the coast-line is such that sheltered landing places cannot be made available, it may be necessary to make arrangements to float supplies ashore when the weather is too bad for landing craft to use the beaches.

29. Arrangements for landing water, if required, will be similar to those during the landing of the assaulting force. The navy's responsibility for conveying water ashore would be taken over by the Board of Trade authorities if and when they take over control of the landing. Should an adequate supply of water not be available in the area of operations subsequent to the landing, the availability of water at an advanced base or some other accessible source of supply will be an important consideration.

Section II.— LANDING FURTHER MILITARY AND/OR AIR FORCES

30. The problem of landing large military or air forces for offensive operations subsequent to the seizing of a covering position is essentially similar to the problem of landing supplies and reinforcements for the assaulting force, and whenever such forces are being disembarked by means of landing craft the same instructions would apply. Owing, however, to the large number of vehicles and the great weight and bulk of supplies required by an army and air force in the field, it may be impracticable to provide sufficient landing craft to enable these forces to be landed fully equipped in the time that can be allowed. If this is so, it must be accepted that these further forces must be

landed with a modified scale of equipment and transport, and that they will not be able to advance any distance inland until either an already organized port has been seized or port facilities have been improvised in a harbour which can be covered by the forces already ashore.

31. The question of seizing or cutting off a port has already been mentioned in connection with the general military problem (see Chapter 18, para. 17), and may be an important feature in the plan of operations as a whole.

32. The possibility of improvising a port will depend mainly on the existence of a harbour with deep water sufficiently close inshore. The essential feature of such an improvisation would be the construction of piers or quays to which transports, lying alongside, can discharge tanks, guns, M.T. vehicles, aircraft, etc.

33. An exception to the general principle, that the landing of a large force calls for the establishment of shore anti-aircraft defences and possibly for port facilities, is the case of a force engaged in an outflanking operation. The outflanking force once landed might rely on joining hands with the force holding the enemy in front, and might thereafter use the lines of communication already established. Such a force would consist almost entirely of fighting troops, and once a covering position had been seized by the assaulting force the main body might be landed rapidly with a minimum of supply and transport and without waiting for the landing of anti-aircraft defences other than those normally accompanying the fighting troops.

Section III.—SUPPLYING AND REINFORCING THE FORCES ALREADY LANDED, WITHOUT INSTALLING AIR DEFENCES

AT THE POINT OF LANDING

34. When the landing operations are on a small scale in relation to the war as a whole, it may be that enemy aircraft, assumed to be in a general inferiority to our own, will not think it worth while to attempt heavy attacks on the communications of the forces landed. Under these conditions the establishment of a complete system of anti-aircraft defences will be unnecessary, ships' anti-aircraft guns sufficing for protection. With operations on a small scale it may even be possible to safeguard the supply arrangements by landing all supplies by night, the ships engaged being kept at sea during the day.

Section IV.—RE-EMBARKATION

35. The general procedure for effecting a re-embarkation will apply equally to the premeditated re-embarkation of a raid or diversion and the re-embarkation in the event of failure.

36. Plans for re-embarkation if the landing fails to meet with the requisite measure of success should be arranged at the same time as the plans for the landing itself. Knowledge of these plans should, however, be restricted to those who prepared them and possibly a few selected subordinates until such time as there is a clear probability that they may have to put into operation.

37. Re-embarkation soon after a landing and evacuation of a hostile shore at a later stage both depend for their success on surprise, steadiness of the troops, good staff work, favourable weather, and an adequate number of craft and transports.

38. The sequence of events in an evacuation is the re that for a landing. In a hurried re-embarkation there will be the opportunity for detailed orders, as time will not allow these to be got out to the troops. Much of the material, many animal possibly guns and aircraft may have to be abandoned in on get the troops away without severe loss. In a deliberate evacuation it should be possible to embark or to destroy everything of me importance, provided the weather holds good and the enemy can be deceived.

39. The rear guard will correspond to the assaulting force in a landing. It must be active and aggressive in order to lull hostile suspicion and to make the enemy cautious in following up.

40. Naval guns and aircraft operating from carriers or air stations in friendly territory can be of great assistance in covering the final stage of re-embarkation.

41. If possible re-embarkation should be carried out in the following order :—

    (i) Stores.

    (ii) Vehicles.

    (iii) Artillery ammunition wagons and air force vehicles.

    (iv) Cavalry.

    (v) Artillery.

    (vi) Infantry.

    (vii) Armoured fighting vehicles.

42. The provision of assembly positions is as necessary for re-embarkation as for disembarkation. In a re-embarkation an assembly position serves as a waiting place to which units must be directed when on their way to the beach. Each assembly position should be placed under the command of an officer selected for the purpose. This officer should be provided with a suitable headquarters and with signal communication to the beach. He should keep the P.M.L.O. informed as to the units and numbers available for embarkation. The M.L.O. will then direct units to be sent to the embarkation points as required by the P.B.M.

43. In deliberate evacuations all movements of troops to the beach and their embarkation can be arranged on a time schedule. The success of this depends, however, on whether timings can be communicated to the troops, and whether they can hold their ground until they are timed to move to the assembly positions. It may require a high standard of devotion and skill on the part of the rearguard to enable this to be done.

44. In framing military re-embarkation orders, it must be remembered that while re-embarkation of infantry is comparatively easy, that of horses, vehicles and stores is more difficult than their disembarkation. At low tide, or after dark, the re-embarkation of guns, wheeled transport and horses is an exceedingly difficult operation, and with an ebb tide off a shelving beach almost impossible.

45. For this reason, it will generally be necessary to send back all guns, transport and horses in time to be embarked when the tide is high, if the requirements of secrecy permit, before dark. In certain circumstances unless guns and transport can be embarked in daylight they may have to be sacrificed.

46. When all except the rear guard are re-embarked the assembly positions should be closed. The officer commanding the rear guard will be informed when this has been done, and he will be told how many boats or lighters are waiting for his troops and where they are. The rear guard will then withdraw from their final position under cover of darkness, or smoke, or naval gun fire, and will move direct to the beach and re-embark.

47. Naval guns should be ready to shell the approaches to the beaches as soon as the last troops have re-embarked in the boats, but whether the guns will actually open fire depends on whether the enemy makes any attempt to interfere with the re-embarkation.

48. It will be the duty of air forces to assist in covering the retirement. If present in sufficient strength they may be able, not only to protect the troops and boats from air attack, but also to harass and delay the advance of the enemy.

SOURCES

CHAPTER 1

US Military Intelligence Service, *German Coastal Defenses*, Special Series No. 15 (15 June 1943)

Naval Staff (UK), Training and Staff Duties Division, *Manual of Combined Operations*, C.B. 3042 (Admiralty, Air Council, Army Council, 1938), National Archives DEFE 2/709

CHAPTER 2

US Navy, *Landing Operations Doctrine*, FTP 167 (Government Printing Office, Washington DC, 1938)

US War Department, *Landing Operations on Hostile Shores*, FM 31-5 167 (Government Printing Office, Washington DC, 1941)

Naval Staff (UK), Training and Staff Duties Division, *Manual of Combined Operations*, C.B. 3042 (Admiralty, Air Council, Army Council, 1938), National Archives DEFE 2/709

CHAPTER 3

US War Department, *Tactics and Techniques of Airborne Troops*, FM 31-30 (Government Printing Office, Washington DC, 1942)

Air Ministry, *Parachute Training Manual* (Air Ministry, London, 1944)

RAF, *Glider Manual* (No.1 Glider Training School, Thame, 1942)

CHAPTER 4

HQ of the Commander in Chief, US Fleet, *Ship to Shore Movement* (US Government Printing Office Washington, 1943)

Naval Staff (UK), Training and Staff Duties Division, *Manual of Combined Operations*, C.B. 3042 (Admiralty, Air Council, Army Council, 1938), National Archives DEFE 2/709

CHAPTER 5

US War Department, *Landing Operations on Hostile Shores*, FM 31-5 167 (Government Printing Office, Washington DC, 1941)

US Military Intelligence Service, 'How British deal with road craters, obstacles', in *Intelligence Bulletin* (August 1943)

US Military Intelligence Service, 'How the Germans Fight in Wooded and Broken Terrain', in *Intelligence Bulletin* (January 1945)

Naval Staff (UK), Training and Staff Duties Division, *Manual of Combined Operations*, C.B. 3042 (Admiralty, Air Council, Army Council, 1938), National Archives DEFE 2/709